TOUCHING
EARTH

For Julia Casparty,
May your gardens
will thrive,

TOUCHING
EARTH

JANET
LEMBKE

All best wishes,
Janet Lembke

Drawings By Joe Nutt

Bb

BURFORD BOOKS

Printed in the United States of America.

10 9 8 7 6 5 4 3 2 1

Library of Congress Cataloging-in-Publication Data
Lembke, Janet.
    Touching Earth / by Janet Lembke.
        p. cm.
    Includes bibliographical reference (p.).
    ISBN 1-58080-088-2 (cl.)
        1. Vegetable gardening. 2. Lembke, Janet. I. Title.

SB321.L462001
635—dc21   00-069667

IN MEMORY OF BILL AND JOE,

FATHERS AND FARMERS

CONTENTS

ACKNOWLEDGMENTS / 9

ROOTS / 13

LAND / 29

PLANTING BY THE MOON / 43

THE LIVES OF THE VEGETABLES / 55

FULL OF BEANS / 73

PARSLEY, SAGE, ROSEMARY, AND LEMON THYME / 91

HIGH SUMMER: ANTAIOS'S CHILDREN / 109

QUEEN MAB'S WAGGON / 131

A BLOOMING OF GARDENERS / 149

FEASTS / 181

TOUCHING EARTH / 201

APPENDIX: SELECTED SEED COMPANIES / 213

NOTES / 215

BIBLIOGRAPHY / 219

ACKNOWLEDGMENTS

As always, I'm grateful to many people for the help that they've given toward getting my adventures with vegetables into readable order. Some, including the shades of Pliny, John Gerard, and Thomas Jefferson, are named in the text. Others have played a quieter though equally consequential role. Among them are:

JEFFERY BEAM, poet and botanical librarian, who has kept me straight on what's native and what's not

TOM GLASGOW, cooperative extension agent, who responds quickly and informatively to the most outlandish queries

JEANNIE KRAUS, botanist, who knows the weeds and wildflowers upside down and inside out, which is frequently the way in which she receives them from me

AKIRA SAKURAI, who knows by heart the ways of isopods, especially sea roaches

There are two others without whom I could have accomplished nothing: my editor, Peter Burford, and my good husband, the Chief. To all of you, my happy thanks.

Fortunatus est ille deos qui novit agrestis—

Panamque Silvanumque senem Nymphasque sorores.

VIRGIL, *Georgics,* BOOK I, 493–4

Blessed is he who comes to know the garden gods—

Pan and old Silvanus and the sister Nymphs.

JUSTAMERE FARM
WICKLIFFE, OHIO

COLUMBUS COUNTY COURTHOUSE
WHITEVILLE, NORTH CAROLINA

ROOTS

NORTH FOR THE WINTER, south for spring, summer, and fall—
that's not how the birds do it. So my husband, the Chief, and I have
been accused of making wrong-way migrations annually since 1984,
the year that we married. We winter in the rolling, mountain-guarded
Shenandoah Valley and drive south in early spring to the flat-as-a-
flounder Carolina coast. There the wide and salty River Neuse flows
not seventy-five feet from our front door, and from the back door we
look out over a loamy, two-acre field surrounded on three sides by an
old hedgerow. It's the river and the loam that count significantly as
an enticement. The truth is that in one vital respect we're not a whit
different from the birds: We travel to where the food is. The river
brings fish and a heart's contentment of blue crabs. The sandy loam
brings vegetables enough to eat fresh and to put up in jars or freezer
pots, which then provide us with summer's bounty throughout the
winter. And these stories grow as surely from that soil as do the
tomatoes, beans, and butternuts.

To grow vegetables means touching earth, a potent metaphor for
renewing strength in all endeavors. People have known of its power

forever. As hunter-gatherers, we honored the trees and vines that brought us nuts and grapes; we revered the woods, mountains, and waters that gave shelter to the deer, bears, peccaries, geese and song-birds, fish and oysters that fed us. When we climbed out of our biologically ordained niche and learned to tame plants and animals some twelve to fourteen thousand years ago, the connection with earth was maintained and still seen as sacred. The word *religion* comes from the Latin *religio,* which means "I reconnect, I bind myself once again." For reconnecting, what could be better than the annual homage to the garden gods, to Pan and the sweet sisters and old Silvanus, who watches over fruit trees? What could be more elemental than observance of the rites of soil and seed? Touching earth is a profoundly religious act.

It is also an act capable of restoring vitality, of healing. Myth makes significant acknowledgment of earth's power to revivify. Once upon a time beyond ordinary time, the ancient Greek hero Herakles was set twelve tasks that called upon all his ingenuity and powers of endurance. Obediently bowing to the mandates of the gods, he rid the land of a man-killing lion and the monstrous many-headed Hydra. He captured a sacred deer with golden antlers, slew a great flock of predatory birds that shot people down with their arrowlike brass feathers, and cleaned a king's dung-choked stables by diverting two rivers to flow through them and carry the filth out to sea. One task bade him travel to the far Hesperides, where the giant Atlas bore the earth upon his shoulders; there Herakles was to take the golden apples that grew upon a dragon-guarded tree. On the way, however, he ran into a daunting roadblock: the kingdom of another giant, Antaios, son of Earth and Poseidon, god of the oceans. To honor his father, Antaios had committed himself to an ongoing construction project: a temple made of human skulls. If anyone was foolish enough to try to end the slaughter, Antaios would decapitate him forthwith and add yet another head to the store of building blocks. No one had ever prevailed against him.

In order to proceed to the Hesperides for his next divinely ordained task, Herakles had to find a way to overcome this murderous obstacle. With confidence in his own superhuman strength, he engaged the giant in a wrestling match. Antaios fell again and again but each time, no matter how bruised and bloody, he rose to fight anew; nor did his strength wane but rather seemed to increase. Herakles, growing weary, guessed at last that the source of Antaios's tirelessness was his mother, Earth. Each time the giant fell and touched her with his body, she infused him once again with her unceasing vitality. Then Herakles summoned the last of his own strength to hold Antaios high above the ground. There, torn from his mother's revivifying embrace, the giant died.

Clearly, Earth plays no favorites. She nurtures weeds, including tyrants, dictators, and noxious giants like Antaios, at least as readily as she sends forth vegetables and bright, bee-summoning flowers. Bane lives side by side with beauty. But the myth's important maxim is this: Touching earth is a prime way to find and regain strength. And that goes for all of us, from beans and bean beetles to human beings. I regret to my core that many people are willy-nilly separated from earth by lifeless things, by steel, concrete, and plastic, high-rise apartments, city streets, and supermarkets. In such circumstances the connections between food and its sources are often obscured or altogether hidden. The rites of reconnection are absent from daily life.

To touch earth is indeed to tap strength. Over the years I have discovered that I can take sorrow or anger to the garden and rub their raw edges smooth, at least for a little while. The long but faltering marriage, the loss of a grown child to cancer—earth has given me solace for these. When the future seems bleak and empty, planting a seed expresses faith in a brighter tomorrow, one that, in only a few weeks, yields crunchy wax beans and tomatoes that the sun has made as warm as flesh. Then, the work of the garden is so direct, so tactile and solid, that it puts doubt and anguish aside for the moment. And picking and processing the garden's bounty offers the enormous pleasure of instant gratification; nothing long term about it, beans harvested in early morning rest in the freezer by noon, and it takes only a short two hours to fill jar after jar with sweet red tomatoes. Weeds, of course, are excellent substitutes for all that riles me, and giving them the Herakles treatment—yanking them rudely from their mother earth—is hugely satisfying. Best of all, the garden brims with life—not just that of the vegetables but with birdsong and insect-scurry. It gave me a counterpoint to the dying marriage, the dead child. It gave surcease to grief and restored my calm. Now I garden for the gritty, sweaty, heart-soothing joy of it and for the ways in which it returns my joy—the sheen on an eggplant's skin and the warmth of a tomato that's been cradled in the sun's hand.

Both the Chief and I tend the vegetables. For both of us, the urge to mess around with dirt and vegetables is rooted in our childhoods. The Chief's involvement began long before he was old enough to have a say in the matter. These days you'd call it child labor, but in those days just before and during World War II any farmer's son old enough to walk—and fear a stern parental hand—was expected to help out with the chores. And chores there were, for the Chief's father, Bill, who worked two outside jobs, as post office janitor and tool setter in a sawmill, also had his own business on the side:

supplying market vegetables to the grocery stores in and near Whiteville, a town of about six thousand souls located in southeastern North Carolina. He farmed four separate truck gardens, all located in downtown Whiteville, just a block away from the town's main street. One garden lay in back of the family's house on a lot at the corner of South Lee and Columbus Streets; today the offices of the *Whiteville News-Reporter* are situated there. A second garden occupied the lot across the street to the east. Two adjoining plots catty-corner across South Lee from the house completed the garden; they're now the site of a tobacco warehouse (but likely won't be for long, given tobacco's lethal nature). Together the four pieces of land comprised six acres. Bill didn't own any of them but rather rented them and paid the rent in produce, an arrangement that was not uncommon back then. Aside from which, as the Chief tells it, Bill was always long on heart and diligence but short on cash.

Why, with two other jobs, did he go in for vegetable farming? The reasons were three, not least of which was nostalgia. He'd grown up on a farm, one that had been in the family three generations back but had been lost to extravagance and carousal. His parents had lived on that land as scratch-dirt tenants, growing cash crops like corn and tobacco. As a grown man, Bill wanted to touch earth again. A second reason was that the extra money brought in by truck gardening went a good way toward helping him support a wife and five children. Last, while the Second World War raged and gasoline for civilians was in such short supply that it was strictly rationed, growing vegetables on a commercial basis entitled him to unlimited supplies of fuel for his truck and car. Just what did he grow? Green beans and limas, collards, okra, tomatoes, bell peppers, corn, brussels sprouts, rutabagas, and just about every other green-growing plant offered on the seed racks of the local farm bureau. He also set in a heap of strawberries and sometimes grew muskmelons. And once he'd found a winner, Bill would save its seeds for the next year's crop. He decided what to put in by checking out the grocery stores to see which kinds of produce commanded the best prices. Some, like tomatoes, corn, and collards, were staples, always in demand. The fling with wax beans, however, lasted for only two seasons because, as it happened, the people of Whiteville simply did not cotton to the color and wouldn't purchase those lemony yellow beans, although they certainly bought an abundance of other varieties, and not just green ones but some that were purple red. After the rent was paid, three-quarters of the harvest was sold to the groceries, while the family ate the rest.

The Chief remembers being rousted out of bed at the hour he calls "dark-thirty"—four-thirty or five A.M.—to go out in one or another of the gardens to perform stoop labor. He was all of five years old when he first went out to sow the seeds or pick the crops. His sister was exempted from outdoor labor, but he and his three big brothers, none much older than he, would gather whatever was in season until it was time to go home for a quick breakfast before school. The sowing of seeds was reserved for him, and him alone, for, as the youngest of the five, he was still very much a "growin' boy," and the seeds by some green magic would grow right along with him. Moon magic was also involved—root crops put in as it waned and the others on its waxing. In summertime, of course, there was no reprieve from garden work, and the picking could last all day long. Or if nothing needed to be picked, bushels of beans waited to be stemmed or shelled so that his mother could put them up. "When I saw those baskets full of work, I got real good at jumping the fence," the Chief says. But when he was caught ducking out, what then? "That belt—Dad would take off that broad belt he wore and tear up my ass. Needless to say, I kept on jumping."

Not all the labor occurred at home. The Chief was often sent during the war years and afterward to a sort of summer camp at Uncle Wilbur's farm, which was located about sixty miles away in Duplin County. Wilbur's forty-odd acres were devoted not just to truck gardening, including three acres of watermelons, but also to tobacco, corn, and hogs. The tobacco fields presented the hardest chores. The Chief and his cousins were sent out to pick the sand-lugs, the leaves closest to the ground, because they themselves were closer to the ground than a grown man. They also cropped the higher leaves, topped the plants of their blossoms, loaded the mule-driven sleigh with leaves to be pulled to the curing barn, and rid the plants of tobacco hornworms. Those grossly corpulent green caterpillars were plucked off by hand, put into a jar filled with kerosene, and then incinerated. Wilbur also had a belt, a thin one that inflicted more hurt than Bill's broad version. But the young 'uns were fed heartily, and Wilbur's wife, Mildred, was generous with hugs. Nonetheless, work at Wilbur's made the work in Whiteville seem less onerous.

Once Bill's belt was applied for an offense that turned out not to be one. All unaware, the Chief-to-be had committed an act of mongrelization. In April 1942 he dutifully took up the bags of seeds, one each of tomato and green bell pepper, that his father had placed at the heads of two adjoining rows. Altogether, the seeds were enough to plant four two-hundred-foot rows. And plant he did, putting tomato seeds in the first and third rows, peppers in the second and fourth. June brought forth a most curious crop: topers, or pepatoes, as they might be called for lack of better names. They were the vegetable equivalents of those lion-tiger crosses called tiglons and ligers. They were, Lord have mercy, hybrids. And the very word *hybrid* comes from a Greek word meaning "outrage." How had such an ungodly thing happened? The moment Bill's eye fell on those fruits that looked like tomatoes on the outside but were the color of a green bell pepper, he knew they were unsalable freaks. Off came his broad belt.

When I first heard this tale, it strained credulity. But then, just as lions and tigers are both cats, tomatoes and peppers both belong to the Solanaceae, the nightshade family. Crosses like these are only highly improbable rather than flat-out impossible. And a newspaper clipping, now yellowed and crumbling, confirms the story. In all likelihood it was locally written, but family legend attributes it to the *New York Herald Tribune,* in an issue that appeared sometime during the summer of 1942. The clipping resided in Bill's wallet till the day he died; the Chief's mother thought that he should have it because, after all, he'd been the perpetrator. Fifty years later the clipping is far from complete; some two column-inches remain, and the edges are tattered. I've put brackets around both reasonable guesses and lost wording.

> [WHAT] IS IT CALLED
> It looks like a tomato.
> Its color is like that of green
> [pepper] and the odor is that
> [   ] and W. A.
> [Stanley], 305 S. Lee Street,
> [say]s the vegetable is a cross
> between the California Wonder
> pepper and the Rutger
> [tom]ato.

[   ] unusual vegetable came
from a pepper vine planted
close to and grown with a tomato bush. The contours of
[the] vegetable are those of the
tomato but the green color
[is that] of a bell pepper.
    Mr. Stanley exhibited one
of the vegetables and said [that]
[the]re are others [   ]

Family memories also insist that the seeds of this fabulous whatzit
were bought by W. Atlee Burpee himself, though the Burpee
Company, which keeps meticulous records of its introductions, can
find no mention of it. Yet a sale did take place, and Bill received a
check for a thousand dollars, a fortune in those days. The Chief recalls
sitting at the supper table listening to his parents talk excitedly about
how to spend this windfall. Part of it was used to purchase a green
1939 Pontiac. Bill never apologized for the whipping. The Chief's
farmwork proceeded as usual.

He finally leaped unreachably over the fence by joining the navy
at the age of eighteen. You'd think that he'd never have gone back as
a grown man to anything so burdensome as growing vegetables. Yet
those years of getting up before dawn to plant and pick, those endless
summers of stemming and shelling, of cropping and topping and
hornworms, made an indelible imprint. Putting hands on and in the
earth became as necessary as sleep and breath. And his children were
led to vegetable gardening as soon as they could walk. He showed
them how to put seeds in the ground and shared with them the

green miracles of sprouting, the chores of weeding and watering, and the robust flavors of the harvest.

My own introduction to vegetable gardens and farming in general also occurred at a tender age but came in quite another fashion from the Chief's. He knew the reality; I met the idea. My father, Joe, owned a play farm not far from the banks of Lake Erie just east of Cleveland, Ohio. I don't know precisely how the word *play* became appended to the enterprise, but that's what I heard from grown-ups early on, before I'd reached an age for analysis. It meant several things, most obviously that the farm was a place for recreation; from the time my father was a little boy, it had furnished him and his family with a second home in summertime. It never provided them with any part of their livelihood. Then, less obviously, the farm served my father as a magnificent toy—and one of his very own—from World War I days until eight years after his discharge from army service during World War II. He was given the farm in 1915, when he was six years old. And the gift came to him this way: When my father's father, who had left a Pennsylvania farm behind in his late teens to settle in the big city and make his fortune, heard that his namesake, young Joseph, wished to grow up to be a farmer, he would have none of it. He himself had escaped the scratch-dirt life to make an honorable place in the world of banking. But the small boy must have given his father no peace; he must have begged and wheedled, and perhaps he cried. To stanch the importuning, the play farm was purchased and presented to the child.

They coyly named it Justamere Farm. It was not without respectable size—fifty-four acres, complete with barns, gardens, pastures, orchard, pond, and icehouse. And it held many of the other appurtenances of a working farm. The lower floor of the cow barn provided living space for five or six Jerseys and Guernseys, plus three draft horses and, for several of my young years, a pony named Midnight. Alfalfa, timothy, and tiger tabby cats, always with kindles of kittens, occupied the haymow on the upper floor. The barn called the horse barn, which had stabled riding and carriage horses at the turn of the nineteenth century into the twentieth, held no animals in my day but was rather filled with bales of straw and barn swallows that yearly built mud nests to brood and fledge their chittering young; its loft was a place for storing useful things like onions and things no longer used but too good to throw away, like a sidesaddle, a martingale, and other antiquated tack. A long, low three-bay garage housed disk, harrow, and other horse-drawn implements; after World War II, it also provided a roof for the newly acquired tractor. There was a chicken coop, to be sure, and a sheep shed that sometimes, according to my father's fancy, housed goats. Nor was the acreage without a strong man to do all the work that my father's family couldn't, or wouldn't, handle— plow the garden, cut the hay, shear the sheep, milk the cows, and tend to the myriad other tasks that keep a farmer busy from dawn to dusk in every season of the year. A sturdy cottage for the farmer, his wife, and two sons stood across the dirt farm road from the chicken coop. And two other houses stood on the farm. One was a mid-nineteenth-century frame dwelling of no architectural distinction, but it was reputed to have been a stop on the Underground Railroad. In the decade before World War II my parents used it for weekend house parties; in my own days on the farm it was rented to a longtime tenant.

But when my father and his family came out from Cleveland in the 'teens and the '20s to spend the summer at Justamere, they did not stay there but rather lived in the Big House, a capacious dark green Dutch Colonial with servants' quarters on the second and third

floors. Grazing sheep mowed its four-acre front lawn. A matching
Dutch Colonial tower held a water tank that served the entire operation, houses, barns, gardens, and all. I remember the noise made by
the pump as it pulled water up from a deep well—*THUNKa-
THUNKa.* That sound, livening the sultry days of summer, seemed
to me an announcement that all was well with the world: Soon the
grown-ups would let me and my younger brother put on our bathing
suits, and they would turn on a sprinkler for us to jump through. But
I spent little time there before the war. My parents lived in their own
house in town and, after I was born, no longer accompanied my
father's father, mother, sister, and servants on their summertime visits.
My father would drive us out from town in his Model A to see them
during the day. Sometimes we'd spend the night; I'd sleep in the comfort of a screened-in porch with trumpet vines growing up its columns.
I remember the tenor of those fairly ceremonial occasions. The cook
and maids, accompanying the family as usual, were ever set to tasks
unlike those they performed in my grandfather's manorial house in
town. The cook had to cope with an icebox that held real blocks of
ice; the upstairs maid and the downstairs maid took turns churning
butter. Everybody picked blackberries, from which the cook made
preserves for spreading on fresh-baked bread. I am reminded now of
Marie Antoinette playing shepherdess at Versailles, but back then I
saw it as a pleasant outing in the country, which brought all sorts of
hands-on delights—cows and calves, downy chicks, bold bantam
roosters, baa-ing lambs, and all the kittens a small girl's heart could
possibly desire. My palate still remembers the odd springtime taste of
fresh, unpasteurized milk after the cows had been put out to pasture
and gotten into the onion grass. World War II and the death of my
father's father in 1945 put an end to such family vacations.

But on my father's return from the war, my immediate family—parents, two brothers, and two hound dogs—moved full time to Justamere Farm. There we munched out on corn, beans, and scallions not two hours out of the garden. There we all drank unpasteurized milk yielded by Bessie or Carmel under the farmer's persuasive hand and also, reluctantly on the part of the children, ate the dairy animals that had far outlived their prime. One question arose every time beef appeared on our table: Is this old cow? And there on the farm, because of the garden, I learned to drive. I was fourteen, two years shy of the age for legally obtaining a license.

With his own convenience uppermost in mind, my father put me behind the wheel of our Ford woody wagon and taught me how to start, stop, and shift gears. The reason: I could then drive the two-tenths of a mile on the dirt farm road to the truck garden, which must have covered a good fifteen acres and did supply some of its crops to local stores. My job was to pick and transport vegetables for the delectation of family friends, who'd make weekend excursions to the country for fresh air and fresh food. For the sake of putting that wagon in motion—the sake of feeling grown up—I'd go to the garden without being asked twice. I'd gather twelve dozen ears of corn or several pecks of the vegetables that were in season, load them into the wagon, and drive back to the Big House. I'd also drive to the garden for weeding sessions, which, as I look back, were not at all perceived as exercises in touching earth but rather as chances to put on a halter top and bare my back for a good suntan. Pulling weeds also afforded an opportunity to pop baby green beans into my mouth or pig out on tender raw peas. My father did not allow me to apply for a license, however, until I'd had a course in driver's ed; that moment finally occurred the summer after my first year in college, which was also the year in which suburbia began to overwhelm Justamere Farm. The truck garden acreage was the first to go, laid out in neatly squared-off lots and two streets named Meadow Road and Garden Drive. In the early '50s, after I had fledged and left the nest, my parents sold the remaining land and moved my brothers and my two postwar sisters to a farm in the Shenandoah Valley. It was in no respect a play farm but rather a place on which beef cattle, sheep, hogs for Virginia hams, and market vegetables were raised.

That Virginia farm is now long sold, and I have lived longer than my father, who was only sixty-three when he died. For the last four decades, it has been my pleasure and my passion to grow vegetables. Ohio, Connecticut, Virginia, North Carolina—wherever I have lived, seeds and sets have gone into the ground each spring. The rule of thumb for tomatoes in north-central Ohio is to plant the seeds when the apple blossoms begin to bloom. Much farther south in coastal North Carolina, tomatoes sown indoors in starter pots may safely be put into the earth come the middle of April. My sons showed little interest in anything but the eating of homegrown goods, but my daughters sowed and planted eagerly. In the 1970s the younger (the one whom cancer claimed) would take her carefully tended cucumbers and black-eyed peas to the Norfield Grange Fair, around the corner from our house in Connecticut, and she'd invariably come home with blue ribbons and cash premiums. It was the ribbons that counted; the premiums were so modest that they were nearly invisible. My children now live their own lives, and, as it's turned out, the sons have both married women with dirty hands—women who garden, that is. The daughter-in-law across the street in Virginia grows roses; the daughter-in-law in Illinois has turned her postage-stamp front yard into a haven for plants native to the prairie and now endangered.

How did my early, superficial exposure to leading the farmer's life come to bear fruit? There is a direct connection: my father's immense pleasure in earth's bounty of plants and animals and his recognition that each life, be it that of a tomato, a rooster, a cow, or a human being, is part of a greater whole. In his later days on the Virginia farm, when I was married with children, he ate anything that his land might provide, not just the farm animals and crops but also the rattlesnakes that came down out of the mountain at the back of the farm, the snapping turtles my brothers brought home after a varmint-plinking session at the farm pond, and the woodchucks that he himself shot. My mother gamely cooked them all, once making an omelet of unlaid turtle eggs. She called the pot-roasted woodchuck "wood chicken" so that my small sisters would not be put off their feed; I'm sure, though, that they knew perfectly well what they were eating. My father also introduced me to more than domestic animals and plants and the occasional woodchuck. Like an Adam, he gave me the names of trees and birds. "That's a silver maple. See the deeply cut lobes of the leaf." Or, "Mourning dove, that's what you hear. Look in the trumpet vine—right there in the center—you'll see her nest." And joy would light his face and voice. His life, despite his father's fortune, was not easy but encumbered by illness and alcohol. But whenever he spoke of the earth-rich things that he loved and whenever he engaged himself with the farmer's rounds of life and necessary death, from planting corn to slaughtering hogs, he'd be transported into an almost mystical state of happiness. In times of need I tend the garden to find deliverance from pain, but more and more these days I plant to reconnect and to enter my father's kind of happiness, his huge satisfaction with land and all it grows.

LAND

LAND—THE VERY IDEA IS RESONANT. It speaks of the time that humankind stopped trekking about in search of plant foods and game and settled down. Since then, until the industrial revolution lured landsmen into the mills and factories of cities, the lives of most of us were directed by the seasonal rounds of agriculture and husbandry. From the first moment that people settled down in villages and started farming, there must have been distinctions between the haves and the have-nots, those few who owned the land they worked and the many who were landless laborers. Owning a piece of earth was at one time the source of wealth and enfranchisement. More than that, it shaped the owners' identity—lords, proprietors, and landed gentry. Those who held no land were destined to work for those who did—slaves, serfs, peasants, tenant farmers. Some of the have-nots found freedom in the age of exploration: The whole of the New World—North, Central, and South America, land beyond dreaming of—was up for grabs. Many who took advantage of the offer were hardly conquistadores or recipients of royal grants; often as not they arrived as convicts or indentured servants who made good. The ancestors of the farming family from whom we acquired our land were just such servants, and illiterate to boot.

My surname, the name I married the first time around, speaks of land. As my then-husband explained, it is formed of the German words *Land* and *Pracht* clumped together, with the diminutive *-ke* tacked on at the end. *Land,* of course, is "land," while *Pracht* means "splendor" and "magnificence." The surname is reduced, however, by that diminutive. It throbs not so much with actual magnificence as with potential that, given a certain diligence, the trees on the land will blossom and bear and the animals be fecund. But there is no promise in the name; it tells only of what might be. Nonetheless, bearing it seems to seal the fate set in motion when I was a child: I am captive to land and green-growing things.

In 1983, when I first came to Great Neck Point on the wide and salty River Neuse, the Chief had property on the river but no garden at all. I'd come to visit him partly because he'd enticed me south with reports of birds like pelicans, pileated woodpeckers, and "cranes," which turned out to be magnificent great blue herons. The other, more important reason was that he'd asked me to marry him, *hmpf,* after I'd been most happily on my own for five years. He was a retired navy chief petty officer who seemed companionable enough, but I was not one whit interested in forfeiting my freedom until I'd checked him out most thoroughly. Did he want a cook, a nursemaid, a dancing partner, a bedmate, or a real friend? We talked, we stuffed ourselves with ceremonial food like shrimp and filet mignon, we went dancing at a bar in one of the tourist towns down on the ocean, we walked on the shore in the moonlight and behaved in general like a couple of sixteen-year-olds, though both of us had passed the half-century mark. Not once, in those enchanted days, did the subject of gardens come up.

But the following year, after we'd married, the Chief learned the reason that I'd allowed myself to purchase an old house, one built in 1910, just weeks before I met him. It was not so much the house as its backyard that had caught my fancy. After the end of my first marriage, I returned to the small Virginia town of my growing up. There I lived in an apartment—a capacious apartment larger than most ranch-boxes, for it occupied the lowest level of an old house built on one of the town's steep hills, a site that allowed both sunlight and stars to enter this so-called basement. The windows of the apartment's living-dining room were eight feet tall. In the second year of my tenancy, because I suffered a craving for sun-sweet home-grown tomatoes, I dug a garden in the sloping backyard. The vines produced abundantly, even though squirrels stole some of the green fruit and my landlady helped herself without asking to the ripened variety. It was the latter depredation that turned my thoughts to acquiring a place of my own, one not necessarily safe from squirrels but certainly beyond the landlady's enthusiastic reach. And when the Chief heard of my wish for a tomato garden, he picked up a shovel and hied himself to the backyard of my new old house, where he dug a twenty- by four-foot plot. The digging turned up odd items from the house's seventy-five years: broken willow-pattern china, the porcelain head of a doll, a hand-forged iron scythe. In the cleared earth he planted green bell peppers and 'Better Boy' tomatoes. He may have been tempting fate, hoping for a rerun of the fabulous hybridization of his boyhood days. Both bore well, though there was no mingling of the twain, and the peppers turned into small trees with woody trunks.

That was it. We've not been without a garden since, though the garden is not in Virginia but in the fertile loam of the field, a onetime melon patch, that lies behind our antiquated and immobile mobile home in North Carolina.

The venue is this: Great Neck Point, a land's-end enclave named only on the nautical chart for the lower Neuse. It's situated on the Great Neck Peninsula, which is bounded on one side by the river, on the other by the local portion of the Intracoastal Waterway. When I first came south to see the Chief, loblolly pines, owned by timber companies, forested much of the peninsula. Houses, some of them lived in for generations by the same families, hugged the twelve-mile-long farm-to-market road that leads from Highway 101 to the peninsula's terminus at the Point. When I first drove down that road in 1983, its last three miles were still dirt, and when the rains poured down it became a quagmire that trapped the cars of people silly enough to venture forth. Not even vehicles with four-wheel drive were safe. Those who chose to live in such an isolated place were notably capable, skilled, and self-reliant, able to grow, build, or mend anything. They doctored the sick and on occasion took the law into their own hands, because the county covers considerable territory and the sheriff's men, along with the game wardens, were usually at work miles away. More than that, they possessed a sure intimacy with the four canonical elements: water and earth, air and the fiery sun. I saw them as the kind of people who'd survive, who'd even flourish, should the rest of the world deflate or go out with a bang. Nowadays, when the twentieth century has wheeled into the twenty-first, they still lead fiercely independent lives and tend to cock a snook at city folk. We're part of them now.

No covenants and damned few laws restrict the ways in which life may be conducted at Great Neck Point. We may, if we so wish, play music at a hundred decibels all night; the worst that might happen is a sharp dressing-down by those whose sleep has been shattered. And any manner of outbuildings sprouts up in our yards, from architecturally elegant pump houses for the wells to tumbledown lean-tos and dilapidated trailers used as storage sheds.

Then, take the local animals. At various times our neighbors have raised rabbits by the hundreds; they have penned and fattened pigs named Barbecue and stabled horses, one of which gave birth to a fine little filly in a garage temporarily converted into a barn. At present one keeps a bawling calf. The people at the Point also and without interruption have raised poultry and waterfowl. Several neighbors have dozens of chickens; one lusty and tireless rooster crows, I swear, not only at dawn but also through the darkest hours of the night. Another neighbor owns and feeds a flock of guinea fowl, though I don't think she houses them—they may often be seen wandering in a tight, raucous group a quarter of a mile from home. Great horned owls seem to fancy guineas: Headless carcasses turn up regularly in fields and yards; the feathers are beautifully calligraphed with black on silver. Then there are the mallards. I'm not sure to just whom they belong. But they've been based at a drainage pond in one of the back fields as long as I remember, and, quacking loudly all the while, they waddle through every nearby yard, go paddling on the river, and take to the air in barnstorming flights.

As it was in my early days at the Point, the neighborhood is still divided into two not always peaceable factions—the newcomers and the old-timers. The former have arrived from mainly rural places all over the United States; the latter are the multitudinous descendants of indentured servants from Surrey, who came to these shores in the 1700s. The great-grandparents of the present family came to the Point in the 1890s; in the 1950s their numerous offspring, many of whom still live here, began converting corn and tobacco fields into waterfront lots. A gulf yawned frequently between the Johnny-come-latelies, who'd barged in unaware, and those who'd lived with—and were profoundly, if irrationally, nostalgic for—the hand-to-mouth hardships of the farming days. The old-timers also grieved, I think, for lost youth and opportunities missed; some exhibited the hostile defensiveness not uncommon in people who have grown up near the dirt-poor, white-trash bottom of the social pecking order. The land ownership that had at first liberated the family became the emblem of a constant scramble to make ends meet. It's also the old story of Greeks and Minoans, conquistadores and Mayans, colonists and Indians—the invaders, that is, and those they displace. But the divisions here no longer run so deep as they used to; the animosities have been blunted. We're thankful for that because without a certain amount of neighborly goodwill we might not have acquired the land on which our gardens stand. But more of that shortly.

Old-timers or newcomers, change has overtaken us all in the last decade. The pine plantations that once stood thick along much of the farm-to-market road have been logged and logged again. Some have been replanted, new trees rising like bristle brushes, but others have disappeared forever. With the discovery that real estate, especially on a waterfront, brings in more money than trees can generate, the timber companies have transmogrified the land. New roads, some paved, some graveled, wend their way through subdivisions that have been cleared of everything but sweet gums and scraggly yaupon hollies. Where these streets, lanes, and avenues intersect with the farm-to-market road, signs point to such destinations as Cypress Bay, Sandy Grove, Waterways Edge, and Baytree Landing. On lots of several acres each rise palatial houses. Often as not they're occupied by a couple not yet eligible for Medicare but affluently retired from the upper echelons of corporate life. Subdivision restrictions do not allow these people to keep pigs or chickens in the yard (though it's dubious that they'd want to in the first place). The population along the farm-to-market road has increased by an explosive two hundred percent—so many people, so many new houses that the county has constructed a water tower and laid down lines to bring soft, sudsy-feeling treated water to us down here in the once benighted boonies. The water hookup came our way in 1999.

The people of Great Neck Point are not so homogeneous as those who've been corralled by the developments. Tradesmen, teachers, aircraft mechanics, landscape gardeners, drywall installers, and the military, both active and retired—among us there's lively diversity in education and occupation. And in the people as well, for all ages and stages are found among us, from newborns to great-grandparents. This multifariousness has not changed since I arrived. There's just more of it—lots more—despite the deaths of four neighbors who gave me their stories about how the Point's people exercise a quintessentially American freedom in living close to the fruitful land and the fish-friendly Neuse. Because we were effectively isolated from town and its services, our lives depended on a pair of conjoined commands: Be neighborly (even if you don't like the people next door) and respect the river, which can change in thirty seconds flat from a benign, barely rippling glow to a raging, killing sea.

The big change today is that the neighborhood has grown with the insistent, thrusting vigor of a weed. Self-reliance has been diluted. Strangers who will never be neighbors move into rental properties, stay briefly, and vanish. Traffic increases. Town seems closer.

In 1983, along the private dirt road three-tenths of a mile long that gives access to our homes, there were only a dozen dwellings: six mobile homes, three frame ranch houses, a brick ranch, and two

cottages, one of which was made of an old bus onto which a porch
and adjoining bedroom had been tacked. Of the dozen, six were
used only seasonally or on weekends. Today eight more houses that
are lived in year-round rise in the back field where tobacco grew
until the late '70s. Two trailers have been replaced by permanent
dwellings of truly manorial design, while one has been more modestly exchanged for a doublewide and another hauled away to a
scrap yard. Nor do the additions mark an end to possibilities for
growth: A slew of potential building lots lies vacant and beckoning.
The Point might become as crowded as any close-packed suburb—
except that descendants of the original farming family still own
much of the land. Many of them live outside North Carolina and
visit only when a wedding or a death demands their presence. Some,
however, continue to live in the area. Thanks to one of them, the
Chief and I touch earth; our gardens bloom.

The Chief and I have always made our gardens on the second tier
of lots immediately behind those on the water. We live on the riverfront, along which stretches the first tier; the second lies just behind,
and on the other side of the dirt road yet a third tier reaches to the
woods. Why not garden on the riverfront? Because that land is filled
with pines and sweet gums that provide cooling green shade and
also act to break the force of the river's winds. For vegetables, we
choose the daylong sunshine of the cleared land behind us.

Our place is peculiarly private. Delivery people often have a hard
time finding us, despite the directional sign posted out at the intersection of the dirt road with our grassy lane. It shows the house
number and an angled arrow indicating a left turn onto our land
near the end of the lane. Their problem is that our immobile home
can't be seen from the dirt road. We are concealed by a hedgerow that

grows thick and tangled on three sides of the second-tier field directly behind us. Loblollies, sweet gums, black tupelos, wild persimmons, wax myrtles, shiny sumacs, bay laurels, vines—the variety of species tells us that it's a venerable hedgerow, dating in parts to the early years of the twentieth century. It embraces us like a living screen. Towhees and sparrows scratch for seeds and insects in its shadows; cardinals nest there, and brown thrashers; bobwhites call their name from the tall grasses at its edge. Come September I gather up ripe persimmons, newly soft and glowing like live embers. They are put through the machine I use for making tomato juice: Seeds are expelled from the end while honeyed pulp flows down a chute on the side. Ah, persimmon pudding and persimmon bread!

The hedgerow-guarded field itself is comprised of three half-acre lots, all owned now or formerly by members of the old-time farming family. For several summers in the late 1970s and early 1980s, the entire field served them as a vast watermelon patch; the earth still has a corrugated look—low humps for the rows, with swales between. In the postwatermelon years the field lay fallow, its only crop a gross array of exuberantly untidy, shoulder-high weeds. Mere mowing can't handle this kind of vegetation; it takes a bushhog—or did till very recently.

Our first garden at the Point stood on land not ours but that of generous next-door neighbors, those whose waterfront weekend camp consists at its core of the old bus. It is they who've always helped us set and rehang our gill nets, they who've treated the neighborhood summerlong to Friday-night fish fries, complete with hushpuppies and homemade coleslaw. Asking nothing, acting out of some inborn goodness of heart, they let us till and use a thirty- by thirty-foot patch of land right behind their camp. In recompense we gladly shared with them our bounty. But the time came when their son took a wife and desired a house in sight of the river. Where once our vegetables grew, there now sits a two-story ranch house—two-story because the house proper sits atop a concreted-in workshop-cum-garage that holds not only tools but also a picnic table, an antique Farm-all tractor, and two jet skis (recreational chain saws, the Chief calls them with fitting accuracy).

Luckily, by the time the house was built, goodwill had come into play. The southernmost third of the watermelon field came into the Chief's hands when the woman who owned it died. She was married to Joe, the youngest of the thirteen children born to the farming family. Before cancer killed her, before illness had even clouded her future, the Chief had approached her with a wistful offer to buy her section of the field. And she'd allowed as how that was a workable idea. I think that she agreed to sell partly because we'd come to know her well; she liked to talk—and liked enchanting us with stories of the old tobacco-growing, hard-drinking, moonshine-making days. But no formal offer was made, no deal cut, till after her untimely death in 1993, when Joe decided to honor his late wife's wish. (How appropriate that his name matches that of my father!) Behold, the Chief found himself in possession not only of the southern half acre but also of one full side of the three-sided hedgerow and another piece of nearly half an acre on the hedgerow's far side. I've named that piece Willow Field, and for a good, green reason. Rooted from cuttings given to us by our Illinois daughter-in-law, two corkscrew willows (*Salix matsudana* 'Tortuosa', a species from Japan) are stretching tall and sending forth slender branches that kink and curl and flutter like ribbons in the wind. Three high-bush blueberries of the variety known as rabbit-eye, perhaps because they are so big and round, grow there, too—chest high, laden in early June with large, sweet fruit and in October with scarlet leaves. The piece to the south of the hedgerow became Garden Field in 1994. That spring the Chief laid out and began to cultivate a new garden, a fifty- by seventy-foot giant of a garden. So much space? That's far more square footage than the trailer has, and more than our Virginia house. I thought the man had gone plumb crazy. But we've filled it yearly with beans of several sorts, squashes, tomatoes, bell and banana peppers, eggplants, and other colorful, crunchy comestibles. We've reaped the bounty every summer since.

Garden Field received a guardian spirit in the fall of 1994, after delivering its first crops. In its southwest corner we planted Sally, the Doberman who had accompanied me joyfully day in, day out for ten years, until a stroke did her in. She is buried with the necessary grave goods: her blanket and her supper bowl.

Five years later, in 1999, Garden Field was augmented by New Field, the northern half-acre, which we also bought from Joe. It had belonged to a sister, the one who lives in a big white house on a third-tier lot and keeps the cocky rooster that crows 'round the clock, but she traded the land she had inherited from the farming days to Joe for another piece of property. When she told us that the land was now Joe's, she also scared us with a rumor that he intended to build a ranch-box house right behind us. The rumor was believable, for Joe had already erected ranch-boxes on several third-tier lots. But Joe agreed to sell. Before we closed on the purchase, though, the Chief jumped the gun. He dug and tilled a twenty- by forty-foot plot, set sturdy poles deep into the loam, and strung a wire fence along them from one end to the other. By summer pole limas were well on their way to emulating Jack's legendary sky-reaching beanstalk. And three varieties of tomatoes, grown from seeds, were set out, along with a tiny variety of zinnia with single petals (*Zinnia angustifolia,* "narrow-leaved zinnia").

Only the central portion of the field remains in the possession of one of the farming family, a woman who lives in Virginia but is fiercely nostalgic for the days of mules and moonshine. Joe, his chicken-keeping sister, and the Chief have all approached her with offers to buy. She scowled at my husband and spat, "I'd rather sell it to a jackass." (Actually, she used the N-word, which I find so offensive that I cannot write it.) She turned the others down, too, though perhaps not so rudely. Nonetheless, we shall maintain her portion of the onetime melon patch. No sense in allowing tall, snake-friendly weeds to bristle like a Mohawk haircut down the middle of an otherwise close-shaven enclosure of gardens and lawn. And snakes there are, from innocuous green and king snakes to copperheads and six-foot-long timber rattlers. When New Field became ours, the Chief gave it and the central portion a bushhogged crew cut. Now only a lawn tractor is needed for the job. Because of the hills and swales, riding the mower is like being aboard a ship that rises and falls as it travels through lapsing, surging waves. New Field in its clean, shorn state will soon host pecan trees as well as a garden.

The Chief has a penchant for fruit and nut trees. At the landward end of the garden in Garden Field he installed six dwarf cherry bushes. They produce a sour fruit of the pie-cherry type, and they're tiny. I've picked them on occasion, removed the pits, and laced them with sugar—yum! But I'm not always quick enough to get them before the birds do. Brown thrashers, in particular, like feasting on that tart red fruit. Nor are cherries and blueberries the only fruit bearers that the Chief has planted. He's also put in pear trees along the line between our backyard and Garden Field: three vari-

eties of pear trees, in fact—two 'Moonglow', two 'Seckel', and one
'Douglas'. 'Moonglow', a 'Bartlett' type, is especially splendid; both
trees bore pears—lush, juicy pears with a blush of rose on the yellow
skin—in their very first year, when they stood not much more than
four feet tall. As good fortune has it, 'Moonglow' is self-pollinating
—unlike most other varieties, which need companion trees in order
to set fruit. The Chief also planted two Manchurian apricot trees,
with which he'd had great success in the days before I knew him.
Those planted here grew right merrily, but, for reasons known only
to themselves, neither bloomed until they'd been in the earth for ten
years. Then one decided to put on a grand show, exploding into
masses of fragrant, starlike pink blossoms. Whether there will be
apricots, we don't yet know. I do know that there will be more fruit
trees planted. Deciding on varieties is part of the fun.

Goodness knows we don't need to plant anything at all, not
vegetables and flowers, certainly not trees and shrubs. Our bodily
survival does not depend upon harvesting and putting up a winter's
worth of food. It's rather that using the land and tapping its goodness satisfies some psychic need for fresh air, for breath itself. And
when I plant seeds, I enter my father's joy. The annual rite starts in
January with the arrival of seed catalogs. But there's another moti-
vation: Making gardens on our scrap of land involves us intimately
in the cycles of the natural world. We do not entertain ourselves
with notions of dominion, a pernicious notion that sets us apart
from the rest of creation, but rather get ourselves grubby and sweaty
in the service of tomatoes, cucumbers, and beans, the material man-
ifestations of the garden gods. Tender plants, and we are in cahoots
with every one of them. Both of us—they instinctively, we with
forethought—conspire for growth and continuity.

PLANTING BY THE MOON

PLANTING BEGINS WITH DAYDREAMS. And with hopes made ardent by the brighter-than-life colors, the unblemished fruits and flowers that decorate the pages of the nursery catalogs. Day after bleak January day the Chief beckons eagerly to spring and summer as he peruses the wish books from suppliers like Burpee, Park Seed, The Cook's Garden, Shepherd's Garden Seeds, and half a dozen others. On a pad of yellow legal paper he jots ever-changing lists. What shall we put in the earth? Butternut squashes, tomatoes, and green beans, of course, along with eggplants, cucumbers, and at least two kinds of peppers, bell and banana. What shall we put in as seedlings? What will be started straight from seeds? What vegetables that we've never grown before might be fun to plant, tend, and savor? Might Swiss chard be worth trying? Or rutabagas? Or something not edible but decorative and useful like gourds, especially the kind that can house purple martins?

For me the enterprise is also filled with subterranean questions. What extraordinary events might take place this year? With what manner of wondrous beasts shall we share the garden? Sphinxes, certainly, but what else? A heffalump or a troll, perhaps, or a high cockalorum. And what escapees from the far Hesperides shall naturalize themselves in Carolina soil and bring us golden apples? What noxious, spiny upstarts from Pandora's box? Of one thing I'm sure: In the garden anything is possible. Stories will sprout and flourish or fail, along with the crops.

The decisions are finally made, the 800 numbers called, and the cardboard boxes containing packets of infinite promise begin to arrive. There are flower seeds and seeds for vegetables, though we've ordered only the latter. Seed companies send what they insist on calling "free gifts" to those who order; marigolds or zinnias are by far the most popular, though we've received a sweet yellow columbine and a raging red-hot poker. The Chief shakes the packets before loading them into a larger carton for transport south. They rattle like castanets.

He leaves before I do. First he checks the phases of the moon to see when it might be best to set in the cool-weather vegetables. He believes, as did his father, that shallow-rooted, light-seeking plants —beans, squashes, members of the mustard family like cabbages, and uncountable others—should be planted as the moon waxes, but the seeds of root crops like radishes and carrots should go in as it wanes. Guidance comes from the annual edition of *The Old Farmer's Almanac,* which also lists the moon's astrological signs, its changing position in regard to the Zodiac, and so directs him on the best times to perform the garden's myriad chores: Plant and transplant when the moon occupies Cancer, Scorpio, or Pisces, the water signs; till, weed, and wage war on insect pests under an Aries, Gemini, Leo, Sagittarius, or Aquarius moon.

I see *The Old Farmer's Almanac,* along with a few others not so well known, as a prime representative of the agrarian style of life that held sway from the time of the New World's first North American colonists until the mid–twentieth century. Today the family farm has been bumped aside by corporate agriculture, and cities house more people than do rural places. Since the change from family endeavor to derustication, we've seen two temporary upsurges in individual desires to return to the land—the back-to-the-earth and commune-building movements of the '60s and, nearly forty years later, the looming of Y2K, which convinced some people that the only way to survive the onslaughts of technology was to become self-reliant. But given modern circumstances, the almanac is something like an appendix: It exists, but to what purpose? I come up with two answers. One, of course, is to affirm the belief of the Chief and his soul mates that the world is governed by primordial laws, that moon, sun, and stars will stay in their places, and that the seasons will continue their great rounds. The word *almanac,* which came originally from the Arabic, refers after all to a publication containing meteorological and astronomical data, along with a hodgepodge of assorted information. *The Old Farmer's Almanac's* other grand purpose is the hodgepodge, which offers people like me much entertainment. Aside from calendars, yearlong regional forecasts, and tables on matters such as frosts and growing seasons and the most favorable times for planting various vegetables, it contains a most curious compendium of oddments, some of them practical, the rest as higgledy-piggledy as things tossed into a junk drawer. A modest selection of topics from a recent edition includes apple recipes (apple crumble bars, cider-cooked apple dumplings, maple-baked apples); chicken lore ("To dream of eggs signifies good luck or a wedding. To dream of broken eggs means a quarrel. To dream of many eggs indicates riches."); places where you can compete in eating contests (okra, lobsters, sweet corn, and pickled quail eggs); and home remedies for pets, as well as a chart for figuring out the age of your dog. You can also consult the almanac for mathematical puzzles, how-to tips on reading palms, advice on making measurements with ruler or tape, and a long report on millennial romance. I am enchanted.

As for the Chief, no matter what the moon and stars advise, mid-February is all the longer he can bear a time that comes more and more to seem like exile (albeit voluntary) in the frigid North. In Carolina butterflies are likely, and balmy days. Three hundred fifty miles separate valley and coast: That's one full plant-hardiness zone and a good three weeks of difference in the last frost dates. The growing season at the Point lasts a month and a half longer than that in our small Virginia town. And the first thing that the Chief does after unpacking the car is pop a beer and stroll out to survey the garden. Sometimes the ground is so soggy it can be tilled only with a motorboat, sometimes a nearly arctic wind comes howling off the river, but if the weather's halfway fair and the soil reasonably dry, he'll set right to work with the tiller. The objective is not to prepare the whole two plots but rather to create a cultivated patch just big enough for spring vegetables: cauliflower, broccoli, and cabbages, a festivity of cabbages, red ones and green ones that will mature into round globes and also a green variety, called a sharp head, that's pear shaped with a steeply tapered top. If he manages to finish tilling by four P.M.—and, more important, if the moon is right—he'll get back into the car, drive twenty miles to the nearest garden center, and buy the plants. They'll be set out in rows before supper. The fresh-dug earth smells like a grand combination of humus, moss, and buried treasure.

Oh, the cabbages! Jeffery Beam, poet and botanical librarian, has riddled "A Riddle" with cabbages at its heart:

> Nesting in the ground their green heads
> bobbing in fertile sea-brown
> In their centers a white brain a curvular pearl
> recalling heavy heads under lidded pots
> Of the same emancipated race as sparrows
>
> The cabbages

The cabbages are self-possessed. The cabbages keep secrets, hiding their brains, their pearls, within coarse outer leaves. And it may well be, as the poet imagines, that they lift those leaves like great green wings, rising at night in a flock and flying off when no one is looking. By morning, of course, they have settled back into their earth-bound self-containment. The poet does not mention, however, that the brainy heads of cabbages also hold stories; so do their flowers and their very roots.

Cabbages, broccoli, cauliflower—all belong to the mustard family, which is sometimes called the Brassicaceae, the "cabbages," and sometimes the Cruciferae, the "cross-bearers," because their four-petaled flowers are shaped like a Greek cross, with four arms of equal length. Anciently, cabbages of every sort were credited with working wonders: Headaches, hypochondria, cancers, gout, baldness, insomnia, drunkenness—these and more were alleviated and, on occasion, entirely cured with cabbage poultices and cabbage tonics. All the varieties of cabbage are as close to one and the same as makes no never mind in the view of botanical taxonomists, who have dubbed the whole crew—not just the trio above, but also kale, brussels sprouts, and kohlrabi—*Brassica oleracea,* which simply means "garden cabbage." The reason is that they have descended from the same wild ancestor, prehistorically domesticated by the Celts. Group names were then tacked on to distinguish one from another. Cabbages, be they round green globes or sharp tops, are members of *B. O. capitata,* "garden cabbages that form heads." Cauliflower's group is *botrytis,* "grapelike," to describe its tightly packed flower buds; the common English name comes from the Latin words for "cabbage" and "flower" —*caulus* and *flos.* It's a cabbage that has, in fact, been bred for its flower buds, not its leaves. It's been part of American vegetable patches for a long time, where, in the words of the poet Rita Dove, it shines "greenish-white in a light like the ocean's." And indeed, it came across the ocean: The Puritans who landed in New England, the Quakers who settled in Pennsylvania, the Dutch of New Amsterdam, and the Virginia colonists all brought it with them from home. Broccoli's group is *italica,* "from Italy," though it's actually native to the Near East. The Romans, however, cultivated and savored it in ancient times, and its common name comes to us from Italy—"little sprouts," the plural diminutive of *brocco.* Brussels sprouts belong to the *gemmifera,* the "sprout-bearing" group. As for kale, well, I'll have more to say about that ancient and peculiar cabbage shortly.

When I arrive at the Point, usually no later than the first of March, the plants have begun to take on size, and the earth in the rest of the garden has been turned over at least once. The Chief is out there every day to keep vigil—observing the smallest signs of growth, checking on the asparagus put in several years ago, fixing a steely eye on the white cabbage butterflies hovering over—alighting on—his infant plants. At the first sight of their airy fluttering he reaches for the Bt—*Bacillus thuringiensis*—a bacterium that parasitizes larval insects, including the cabbage butterfly's leaf-green caterpillars. Bt is one of the two pesticides that we use; the other is Sevin. Both are applied lightly, and only in case of real need—the cabbage leaves riddled with great gaping holes, the tenderest egg-plant leaves eaten clear to the stem. It does not do to overdust the plants with poisons, for both larval and adult insects are able to develop resistance to the things that poison them. In the garden survival of the fittest is at work among the pests as well as the plants that we've set in the fertile sandy loam.

In mid-April, when the broccoli and its companions are still three weeks away from harvest, my garden work begins. The threat of frost has gone; spring enters its fullness of bare-armed days and blanket-wrapped nights. My first job is to survey the tools. Out to the shed I go to find the necessary seed-starting pots and trays. Then I gather together the things that are usually put inside with haste before we make our fall migration north: trowel, dandelion digger, rake, sharp-bladed hoe, small three-pronged hand cultivator, and two homi tools, one with short handle, one with long. An imple-ment of Korean name and origin, the homi, made of hand-forged steel and shaped like a sickle, looks primitive—a six-inch, teardrop-shaped blade with a sharp point that's set at a right angle to the wooden handle—but it is in fact a mighty enemy to weeds, especially to grasses with stubborn, wiry roots. It cuts through weedy tangles like a knife through soft butter and even extracts the deep-set bulbs of wild onions and false garlic whole. There in the shed I make sure, too, to unblock the red wheelbarrow, which is stored for the winter behind barrels containing gill nets, and to separate the plastic five-gallon buckets that have been piled one inside the next. The buckets, which once held joint compound used by neighbors who run a drywall business, are invaluable for tasks like stashing weeds before they're put into the refuse pile and toting newly picked vegetables into the house. The best tools of all, however, are readily available at all times; they are not scattered, nor are they blocked. And they are multipurpose—weed pullers, seed tampers, fruit pickers: My own two hands, with plain gold wedding band on the left and a thread-like scar on the right by the carpal joint, where arthritic bone was removed from the base of my thumb. The garden will, I hope, be in good hands.

We keep our eyes on the moon. At its March waxing I put in lettuce seeds at the end of the row of cabbages. When it wanes two weeks later I sow radishes—the round scarlet 'Cherry Belle' and 'Cherry Bomb', both of which develop a good nip; the elongated, sweet-flavored 'French Breakfast', red shading to white at the root end. In the same week I put seeds in starter pots. Trays of pots occupy considerable space on the floor of the back deck: bush cucumber, green bell pepper, eggplant of the plump, ovoid, dark purple kind, and three varieties of tomatoes. Herbs are started, too: marjoram, parsley, thyme, cilantro, and the basil that tomatoes—be they fresh or be they cooked in spaghetti sauce—cannot do without. For a lark, I also try fennel for use in *pasta e fagioli,* the Italian pasta and bean soup. Its primary leaves are long and slender, like narrow wings. When the secondaries appear a few days later, they're as ferny as asparagus or their namesake dog fennel, the former an invited guest in our garden, the latter a permanent squatter that shows up wherever there's space to move in—amid the tomatoes, in the mowed back field, beside the shed.

When it's time to sow the bean seeds directly in the earth toward the end of April and when the potted seedlings are ready to transplant come mid-May, the Chief insists that I become a lunatic and mind the moon. I'm not as true a believer as he is, but there's no harm in abiding by his wishes here, and for all that I know the moon may truly help. In his book it doesn't seem to matter when the starter pots get going, but for putting in bean seeds and setting young, tender plants in the earth, earth's satellite rules. I dutifully wait till just after the new moon. As it waxes, so shall the beans take root and reach for the sun, so shall the eggplant, tomato, and cucumber seedlings plump out, bloom, and set fruit.

My first husband, whose native tongue was German, gave me a mnemonic for looking at the moon and knowing which phase it was in. *Abnehmen* and *zunehmen* are the German verbs for "to wane" and "to wax." *Ab-* means "away," *zu-* equals "to." And when you look at the moon and see that it's rounded on the left like an *a* in script, the first letter of *abnehmen,* then it's diminishing. But if it's rounded on the right like the top of a *z,* the letter with which *zunehmen* begins, it's heading toward the full. And *The Old Farmer's Almanac* adds to my knowledge with a little verse that speaks to the timing of the phases:

> The new Moon always rises at sunrise
> And the first quarter at noon.
> The full moon always rises at sunset
> And the last quarter at midnight.

We're not adventurous gardeners, but we do make forays every year into the realm of *what if*—what if we planted a new variety of winter squash, what if we used carrot seed tapes instead of seeds, what if we grew gourds and set in horseradish.

Horseradish—oh, strong and heady root! Formally, the plant is known as *Armoracia lapathifolia*, "sorrel-leaved horseradish," for its large foliage. Native to eastern Europe, Russia, and Finland, it, like the cabbages, is a member of the mustard family and was prehistorically introduced to the Mediterranean countries. For the Chief and me, it is one hundred percent essential to our diet: Each summer we bring home fifty pounds of shrimp straight off a trawler, but no store-bought seafood sauce delivers enough of that pungent horseradish heat. So the Chief ordered half a dozen roots, puny, twiglike dark brown things, which arrived looking desiccated, if not quite dead. But they hadn't lost their pizzazz; four weeks later their leaves burst forth and rose like big green banners in the southeast quadrant of the plot in Garden Field. The following spring, before the large-leaved plants had begun to flower, I dug up a mess of fat white roots, cleaned them, and ground them outdoors so that fresh air would dissipate their eye-watering, sinus-clearing vapors. The puree was mixed with vinegar and stashed in the fridge for retrieval when it came time for adding the necessary zing to seafood sauce.

Some vegetables, however, we do not—will not—plant: zucchini and other thin-skinned summer squashes, southern staples like okra and collards, and corn of any color or stripe. I'll come to the reasons, a host of them, shortly.

Our garden is eclectic, as a garden should be. The deciding factor on what and how much we plant is, Do we like to eat it? If the answer is Yes, we tend to overdo, planting a hundred feet of beans when fifty would suffice and enough tomato vines to keep me canning night and day for a full month. My Illinois daughter-in-law came to the rescue some years ago with an immensely useful cookbook called *Too Many Tomatoes, Squash, Beans, and Other Good Things: A Cookbook for When*

Your Garden Explodes. Like us, its authors must have been victims of wild enthusiasm.

As I sow the seeds and set out the seedlings, my imagination summons a medieval song about the fickleness of luck when a wandering scholar goes out gambling. *O Fortuna velut luna*, it begins— *O Fortune, like the moon, ever-changing, waxing, waning*.

Radishes, tomatoes large and small, beans of several kinds, peppers, butternuts, cucumbers, eggplants, the many herbs: Filled with hope and desire, filled as well, like the plants, with an instinctive wish to survive, every year the Chief and I go gambling and moon-gazing, taking our great green chances.

THE LIVES OF THE
VEGETABLES

SUMMER IS A-COMING IN; the yellow-billed cuckoo sings loud in the hedgerow. And as I follow the moon's directions, raking sandy loam over seeds, patting it down around the seedlings, the garden and the voices of plantsmen long gone tell me stories. Red, yellow, gold, orange, purple, a dozen shades of green, it's a colorful, wonderfully peaceable international community. Even the vegetables—"weggebobbles," James Joyce calls them—that we, by intention, do not plant are present in spirit, insisting that I attend to their tales as well.

Corn, summer squash, okra, and collards—the unholy foursome—are certainly possessed of noble histories. The last two are Old World plants that crossed the seas, but the squashes and *Zea mays*, "maize corn," are native to the Americas. Our difficulties with them are manifold. To begin with, growing enough corn for both eating and putting up commands considerable garden space, and even then we've found that raising it is at best an iffy proposition. Thomas Harriott, an English scientist and mathematician who accompanied a 1585–86 expedition to the place he called the "new found land of Virginia," wrote in 1588 of the Indians planting "foure graines" of corn in each hole to make sure that one would sprout. An old verse repeats the advice:

> One for the worm,
> One for the crow,
> One for the gods,
> And one to grow.

Then, if one plant does spring up, rise tall, and develop ears and tassels, the crop is still not safe, for the gods of earworms and smut may not have been properly appeased. And oh, there is a god of smut, the god who explodes kernels of corn and turns them into sullen, powdery puffs of black. The Romans called him Robigus and sought to keep his ruinous work at bay by calming him with a festival, the Robigalia, every April. Granted, Robigus was an Old World god, and corn—maize—is a plant indigenous to the New World. But any deity responsible for mildews and rusts, scurfs and blights also has a stake in smut, which affects cereal grains of many kinds all over the planet.

The reasons for keeping the garden zucchini-, okra-, and collard-free have to do with texture and flavor. All, of course, are basically peaceable, innocent, well-bred, and much-admired species, but each presents the Chief and me with a particular problem. Zucchini is formally *Cucurbita pepo* of the variety *melopepo,* which translates redundantly as "gourd melon-squash," and it's a member of the Cucurbitaceae, the gourd family. This squash used to be called cocozelle; the name *zucchini* gained currency only in the 1920s when Californians adopted the word and gave it to the rest of the country. Indeed, the common name is Italian for "little gourd" (but if you are British, you call it a "vegetable marrow"). Whatever it's called, it is the sneakiest of vegetables: If you take your eye off it for a moment, one single moment, before you pick it, it bloats. One writer, whose name is long lost to me, described it as a "pregnant baseball bat." And after cooking, zucchini and the other summer squashes—be they straightnecks, crooknecks, or cymlings—are mushy and notably lacking in taste, unless they've been stewed with gobbets of butter and onions; even then, I think it likely that almost no one would know the difference if the squash were left out entirely. What's more, the summer squashes, unlike the winter sort, are low in nutrition. As for zucchini bread, a slice tastes good indeed, but the flavor is that of the spices, not the squash. Far better to make banana or pumpkin bread, each of which retains the character of the main ingredient.

The problem with okra—*Hibiscus abel moschus,* "edible musk," for its musk-scented seed—a member of the large mallow family, which includes hollyhocks and cotton, is that it defeats me. Okra, the single edible member of its family, is native to Asia, but the name by which we know it comes out of Africa, a heritage from the days of slavery, when it became widely cultivated throughout the West Indies. In the 1820s okra pods sported thorns around the base, and the pods themselves were ribby, narrow, and pointed; these characteristics have been bred out of the plant and a smooth roundness bred in. Okra is also called gumbo, a Bantu word that has slid over to denominate a kind of thickened soup made of vegetables, rice, and various meats, like chicken, hot sausage, or shrimp. Okra is surely a splendid plant to look at—tall as a light post with graceful, deeply incised leaves and purple-centered yellow flowers as large and glorious as those of hollyhocks. Goodness knows, I have lots of opportunities to look at it, for several neighbors at the Point grow it—and not only grow it but add it to their soups and casseroles or batter-fry it with an enviable success. But I've never been able to master the trick of cooking it so that it's dry rather than overwhelmed by its soup-thickening constituent, which one horticultural dictionary euphemistically calls the "jellylike substance" in its pods. *Goo* would be a better word, or *mucilage.* Or *slime.*

As for collards, I'll eat them if no other greens are available, but the Chief flat-out won't, for once upon a time he was too often obliged to eat the stuff—"Clean your plate, or straight to bed with you and no dessert." Collards come from the long, motley line of king cole—the cabbages. The plant in its New World incarnations is an accident, the unwitting result of a cross between cabbage and kale, and it resembles both: cabbage in its broad, smooth leaves, kale in its inability to form a head. Both collards and kale are known as *Brassica oleracea acephala,* "headless garden cabbage." Looseleaf greens are actually the earliest form of cabbage, and they were cultivated long before heading types were developed in the Middle Ages (though the heads then were loose and didn't become pale and compact until the twentieth century). Kale came to America in 1540 with the French explorer Jacques Cartier; in the eighteenth century it was featured in the extensive gardens of George Washington and Thomas Jefferson. The word *kale* comes from the Latin word for "cabbage," *caulus.* As for collards, the common name is a slurring of the medieval English *colewort,* or "cabbage plant," *wort* being a word used to signify an edible or medicinal plant. Collards are cold tolerant and, in the South, have a long growing season, producing fresh greens well into winter. As dependable sources of many minerals, as well as vitamins A and C, they're certifiably nutritious. The trouble with them, so far as I'm concerned, is that to cook away their intrinsic toughness and make them palatable, they must be stewed for hours—stewed to death—usually with a large chunk of salt pork. Even then I find the flavor strong with a bitter aftertaste. Worse, collards contain a mort of oxalic acid, which can create painful crystals in people who over-indulge. (All right, I admit it: These informative tidbits are actually ways of excusing the fact that collards are one of two vegetables that appeal in no way whatsoever to my palate. The other is salsify, also known as oyster plant; though it is highly recommended by classical Greek and Roman authors and was a favorite of my maternal grandmother, my childhood dislike remains strong, and my appetite for the stuff, nonexistent.)

But quirks aside, there are lots of vegetables that we do grow. Many of them were given to the world by the Americas—tomatoes, snap beans and limas, the peppers hot and sweet, and the winter squashes. The word *squash* is a short form of *askutasquash,* the word used by the Narraganset Indians, the tribe that greeted the first European settlers of Rhode Island. Our other vegetables, the cucumbers, carrots, and radishes, the peas, asparagus, and eggplants, are immigrants from around the world. New World or Old, their stories enthrall me.

Eggplant has a curious history. *Solanum melongena,* the "mad-apple nightshade," is native to India but was taken early on to both China and the Near East; it came to Europe by way of Arab traders. Classified botanically as a berry, it was early accepted as edible in the countries surrounding the Mediterranean, but the inhabitants of more northerly lands long bore a deep suspicion of this "apple" that they called not only "mad" but "raging," for they believed that it could poison and possibly kill anyone unwise enough to take a bite.

The 1633 edition of *The Herball* of John Gerard, the English botanist, notes a report that:

> In Egypt and Barbary they use to eat the fruit of *Mala insane* [mad-apple] boiled or roasted under ashes, with oile, vineger, & pepper, as people use to eat Mushroms. But I rather with English men to content themselves with the meat and sauce of our owne Countrey, than with fruit and sauce eaten with such peril: for doubtlesse these apples have a mischievous qualitie. . . . It is better to esteeme this plant and have him in the Garden for your pleasure and the rarenesse thereof, than for any vertue or good qualities yet known.

The fruit with which Gerard was acquainted, the fruit growing in cool-climate English gardens, was "of the bignesse of a swan's egg, and sometimes much greater, of a white color, sometimes yellow, and often brown." It is the white form that inspired the plant's common name (white eggplants the size and shape of goose eggs are available today). But Gerard, I note, does not mention the prickles on the berry's thick green stem and calyx; picking eggplants is easier done with gloves than bare hands. The vegetable was slow to get a start in New World gardens, arriving here in the early nineteenth century, and even then it was grown not for eating but for ornament. A nineteenth-century American recipe for eggplant appears in *The Virginia Housewife,* the 1824 cookbook by Mary Randolph, whose brother married Thomas Jefferson's daughter Martha. She writes: "The purple ones are best; get them young and fresh; . . . cut them in slices an inch thick but do not peel them; dip them in the yelk of

an egg, and cover them with grated bread, a little salt and pepper—
fry them a nice brown. They are very delicious, tasting much like
soft crabs." But not until the twentieth century rolled in did suspicion
abate enough so that the idea of cooking up eggplant could truly
take hold in American kitchens.

Gerard also expresses a suspicion about eggplant's cousin the
tomato, *Lycopersicum lycopersicum*. Each part of this double-barreled
moniker means "edible wolf-peach." Eighteenth-century nomenclators presumably thought that it was inferior to a true peach—a
peach in wolf's clothing. Gerard calls it the "Apple of Love," but not
on the grounds that its berries were intoxicating, not to mention
poisonous. Rather, he assures us that "the whole Plant is of a ranke
and stinking savour" and that its apples "yeeld very little nourishment to the bodie." The fruits of the ancestral wild plant, which
originated in Central America and northern South America, resem-
bled small red currants. They were domesticated and eaten readily
by the precolonial population; the common name we use today
comes from Mexico, where once upon a time the Spanish explorers
picked up the word *tomatl* from the Aztecs. But European botanists,
examining this plant that adventurers and fortune seekers had
brought back home in the early days of exploration, recognized it as
one of the nightshades, a family that includes a host of truly poisonous plants, like mandrake and jimsonweed. The first report of
tomatoes growing under cultivation in the United-States-to-be
came in 1710, noting that they grew in the Carolinas, whence they'd
been imported, most likely from the Caribbean. And Thomas
Jefferson, who gardened on a prodigious scale, grew "tomatas." He
seems to have eaten them, but it took another 150 years for the
fruits to rise wholly above the rumor that they, too, could be fatal.

The rumor may have been based on the fact that, while the fruit is not poisonous, the leaves and stems most certainly are, though not lethally so; they only cause a mighty ruckus in the digestive system. Today tomatoes are the staple sine qua non in many gardens—the old-fashioned indeterminate vine types that keep growing and bearing fruit till first frost, the modern determinate bushy hybrids that set their fruit in a short period of time and cease yielding when it's gone. For the Chief and me, summer comes into its fullness only when tomatoes ripen to rosy succulence and appear on our table—sandwiches at lunch, salad for supper. And when their sweet flush is done, we become abstemious, eschewing altogether the cardboard supermarket sort. The poet Erica Jong doesn't go far enough when she says, "If a woman wants to be a poet, / she must dwell in the house of the tomato." Rita Dove comes closer to the mark when she writes of tomatoes as "good poetry." What I know by heart is that a woman who wants to retain the fruit's red poetry and visit again the lyrical heat of summer must also know how to save love apples in jars.

A third member of the Solanaceae has ever been present in our garden—the mild, crisp, nutritious, and flavorsome bell pepper. Like the eggplant and tomato, it's classified botanically as a berry, and it belongs to the Grossum group, the "large" group, of *Capsicum annuum,* the "biter that grows annually," so named for the tongue- and palate-searing heat in many of its varieties. Native to Central and South America, capsicum seeds have been found there in fossilized human feces and also on the floors of caves in which prehistoric people lived as long as nine thousand years ago. Wild plants must have been used at first, but archaeological evidence indicates that Indians were purposely cultivating capsicums as early as about 4000 B.C. The New World's peppers—explorers recorded both hot and sweet sorts—were transported to the Old World in 1493, within a twinkling of their discovery by Europeans. One hundred fifty years later Gerard, aware of their general origin in the Americas, calls them "Ginnie peppers"—peppers from Guiana, that is—and lists three kinds, distinguished one from another by the shape of their pods or, as he would have it, their cods. He writes of one kind that after its flowering "grow the cods, greene at the first, and when they be ripe of a brave colour glittering like red corall, in which is contained little flat seeds, of a light yellow colour, of a hot biting taste like common pepper, as is also the cod itself." He's right about the brave color but not about the source of the heat, which has been said to cure all manner of ailments, from toothache to cholera, seasickness to the DTs. The heat rises from the compound capsaicin, which retains its strength in the pepper berry for a long time. Fresh peppers, dried peppers, powdered peppers—each kind can burn the mouth or bring stinging tears to the eyes, should an unwashed hand be wiped across them. By burning peppers, Indians released the vapors of capsaicin to repulse the conquistadores. The compound is contained, however, not in the seeds or in the flesh but dwells rather in the placenta, the attachment of seeds to the pod. Hot or sweet, all capsicums are chock-full of vitamins A and C. But it's not hot peppers that we choose to grow. Neighbors produce jalapeños, cayennes, and other gustatory fireworks by the tens of dozens and are glad to donate them in case of need. It's the sweet ones, though, that appeal to us, and sometimes the long lemon-yellow banana peppers are added for their pleasing color. Diced, they give crunch to tossed salads; stuffed and baked, they slide down the gullet as easily as butter. Certainly they are as necessary to homemade spaghetti sauce as basil.

Peppers are children of the light. The garden also contains a few of those that dwell in the dark. The one root vegetable that we always plant is the radish, which originated prehistorically in northern China and from there moved steadily westward into the classical world. Picked, trimmed, and rinsed, radishes explode in the mouth with a cool, crisp pungency. They taste red even when they're white or, with some heirloom varieties, yellow or black. It's been said that the name comes from the Saxon *reod*, which means "red," though the more likely view is that the name is based on *radix*, the Latin word for "root." In its peculiar—one might say "radical"—way, the skin is hotter than the inner substance, a fact that was known of old, and the heat is a product of sulfur compounds. I've never fallen victim, however, to the complaint mentioned by the Roman naturalist Pliny the Elder (A.D. 23–79) in the kitchen-garden section of his *Natural History;* there he credits radishes with a powerful ability to engender belches and flatulence in almost anyone who eats them. *Raphanus sativus*—science uses Pliny's word for the tribe of radish and appends a species name meaning "cultivated." And *raphanus* itself is an old word that indicates redness. Gerard, writing one and a half millennia later, agrees with Pliny about the bad effects of radishes: Eaten before meat, "they cause belchings, and overthrowe the stomacke." But he also gives them credit as remedies for a hodgepodge of ailments, from coughs to kidney stones. Jefferson is silent on the matter of radish-induced indigestion, but it's safe to assume that he savored them, for his meticulously kept lists show that he planted them annually in his vast gardens at Monticello. The truth is that the roots, leaves, and stems of radishes are especially rich in vitamin C. And yes, the leaves and stems have long been utilized as food, though not by the Chief and me.

Another root vegetable, the carrot—*Daucus carota*—is not always part of our year's garden scheme, for though we may sow its seeds propitiously on the waning of the moon, the new-sprouted plants are tiny and easily lost from sight amid the Carolina coast's ferocious weeds. When we do succeed, though, the orange roots are small but sugar-sweet. And they have come to us over the long millennia out of two different places: Europe, for a white form; and central Asia, where gardeners cultivated both a violet and a yellow form before the birth of Christ. But it took till the thirteenth century before these two arrived in northwestern Europe by way of the Mediterranean. In the early seventeenth century John Gerard notes both yellow and red carrots, "pleasant to be eaten and very sweet in taste." Later records characterize the carrot as bitter or tart. The carrots that we now define by their orange color resulted from a cross between the yellow and the violet sorts and were developed in Holland during the late 1600s. It wasn't till the nineteenth century, however, that sweetness became a reliable part of their taste. *Daucus carota*—the scientific name is formed of two Latin words that, translated, sound as if they'd been thought up by someone advertising Little Caesar's pizza. They mean "carrot carrot," as if the root's flavor and crunch—indeed, the whole plant's essential carrotness—need emphasis. Precisely the same binomial denominates that glory of roadsides and old fields, Queen Anne's lace, or wild carrot, which was directly ancestral to the cultivated sort that raises its feathery leaves in our garden, and sometimes its white-flowered umbels (if we've somehow missed a plant amid the other verdure). Gerard says of the wild carrot that it "serveth love matters" and that its root "is more effectual than that of the garden [carrot], and containeth in it a certain force to procure lust." Wild and domesticated, the twins belong to the Apiaceae, or parsley family, which some botanists call the Umbelliferae, the "umbel-bearers," for the plant's typical flowers, which form delicate clusters in the shape of a flat or gently rounded parasol (the words *umbel* and *umbrella* stem from the same root). Aside from parsley—the Latin name of which, *apium,* has been given to the entire family—the tribe includes herbs like dill, cilantro, and lovage; vegetables like celery, parsnip, and fennel; and toxic (though not unattractive) plants like the poison hemlock that did in the Greek philosopher Socrates in the fourth century B.C.

The carrot is a vegetable of truly venerable age, but it looks like a come-lately upstart compared to the pea. Fossilized remains of *Pisum sativum,* the "cultivated garden pea," have been found in the excavations of Swiss lake villages that were inhabited as long ago as 4000 B.C. Just where the pea originated, however, is a mystery— India perhaps, for the root of the word is Sanskrit. It must have been among the first edible plants domesticated when humankind climbed out of its hunting-gathering niche some twelve to fourteen thousand years ago. The Chief plants seeds for our peas in February before I arrive at the Point. "May peas," he calls them, as did his father, for the month that the plumped-out pods are ready for picking. Peas come in an astonishment of varieties—climbers like the earliest peas, bush types, snow and snap peas with edible pods, shelling peas with pods that are discarded. Gerard notes nothing but climbers, both domestic and wild, and that upreaching sort is what Jefferson grew in a host of varieties—'Forwardest', 'Middling', 'Charlton Hotspur', 'Marrow Fat', 'Spanish Marotto', and twenty-five others. Of the grand array of vegetables in Jefferson's garden, peas were his favorite. The Chief chooses a bush-type, shelling pea that can be sown before winter's chill is gone but is also able to tolerate warm weather—and May weather on this coast can range from warm to meltdown. But even though it's a bush type, staying close to the ground, it thrusts forth curling tendrils that tend to grab whatever's handy, be it a neighboring pea plant or a weed. Peas, peas, peas— after the harvest, we devour them; there's rarely enough left to put up for the winter.

I suspect that no asparagus whatsoever will ever be left for putting up once our patch begins to produce. It's a very small patch to begin with. Then, as with carrots, the first leaves are so fernlike and delicate that they're hard to see amid the more insistent greenery, and I've pulled them off without realizing what I was doing until too late. We've had one disaster that could have sent them into never-never land for good: Not long ago, to help us out before we migrated south, a neighbor brought tractor and disk over to Garden Field and did a most excellent job of tearing up not just the earth but also the perennials within it. The small blueberry bushes at the garden's landward end and, to our astonishment, the horseradish did not survive. And horseradish is supposed to have the weed's gift of out-living any catastrophe. But asparagus clings hard to life; its leaves reached sunward later that spring. Come the end of each March in the two years since, they still look for sun. Next year we'll cut a small crop of *Asparagus officinalis,* "edible asparagus." The plant belongs to the lily family, along with the onion, bellflower, and sarsaparilla. For thousands of years, it has pleased human palates, among them that of Pliny, who devoted considerable space in his *Natural History* to the delicate art of their cultivation. The binomial combines *Asparagus,* a classical Greek word that has been latinized, with the term *officinalis,* a Latin catchall indicating that the plant is useful as food, medicine, or both; the name was authorized by the master

taxonomist Linnaeus himself. Calling it "Sperage," Gerard knew it
well; his *Herball* not only describes and depicts the garden and wild
varieties that we know today but also shows a sperage that I'm glad
I have not met, for its stem, like that of a rose, bristles with hard,
sharp thorns. Jefferson sowed asparagus seeds in his garden from
before the Revolutionary War to shortly before his death in 1826;
in his garden books and letters to compatriots he notes frequently
that "Asparagus come to table, Mar. 23–Apr. 14." The dates are just
about a week later than those for Great Neck Point. I do not know
what varieties he planted. Our asparagus of choice is 'Jersey Giant',
and we ordered only male plants, for males will produce for two
decades, while females, reversing the human equation, do not last
nearly so long.

As asparagus loves spring, so do cucumbers love summer. The
hotter the weather, the better they thrive, as long as the soil holds
sufficient moisture. *Cucumis sativus,* the "cultivated cucumber," was
probably domesticated prehistorically in the Indus Valley of northern
India, where it can still be found in the wild today. It was dispersed
into China and the Near East by the seventh century B.C. Along
with the melons, squashes, pumpkins, and eponymous gourds, it's
one of the Cucurbitaceae, the gourd family. Pliny, who finds it a
peculiar though not unpalatable product of the kitchen garden,
reports that the emperor Tiberius insisted on having a cucumber
every day; to appease his imperial appetite, his gardeners made mobile
cucumber beds that could be wheeled out into the sun or covered
with glazed frames on cold winter days. Pliny also ascribes sundry
medical uses to the cucumber: It cures coughs and liver diseases, it
makes a dandy enema, and its seeds provide a surefire antidote to
scorpion stings. Fifteen centuries later Gerard delivers highly detailed

instructions for growing this warmth-seeking plant not just in cool, foggy England but also in the often frigid farthest parts of Scotland: "First of all in the middle of Aprill or somewhat sooner (if the weather be anything temperate) you shall cause to be made a bed or banke of hot and new horse dung taken forth of the stable (and not from the dunghill)." He then gives advice on the depth of soil, the use of cloths or straw to protect the tender plants from "injurie of the cold frostie nights," and the proper method of transplanting seedlings when they have four to six leaves each. He endows the cucumber with a host of medicinal and practical virtues: It is a skin cleanser, a diuretic, and a soothing remedy for inflamed lungs. More than that, it "doth perfectly cure . . . red and shining fierie noses (as red as red Roses) with pimples, pumples, rubies, and such like precious faces." Even in modern times cucumbers have been made into poultices and applied to foreheads, cheeks, noses, and chins as a beauty aid, though it's doubtful that they could ever have taken the sass out of W. C. Fields's dumpling nose or Jimmy Durante's famous schnozz. But neither Gerard nor Pliny mentions the cucumber's vice, namely that some unfortunate souls are so sensitive to its components that eating it causes grievous indigestion, accompanied by copious burping. Neither the Chief nor I have such troubles—no red noses between us, no unwanted eructations. He likes his cucumbers served in slices as thin as if they'd been shaved with a micrometer, while I mix mine with sliced onions, chunked tomatoes, and vinegar—a large, frequently replenished pot that sits in the refrigerator all summer long. We don't plant our seeds in manure, either, but rather in starter pots, then in the sandy loam of Garden Field— but we work in a climate far warmer than that of Gerard. Of all the cucumbers available, from climbers great and small to the little pickling sorts no bigger than a finger and the round yellow heirloom variety called 'Lemon,' our favorite, the one we've planted year in and year out, is a bush type. Square of stem, it sends forth little tendrils, smaller than those of its climbing kin, but it hugs the ground and spreads out neatly like a slightly fuzzy, oversized green table mat. Little star-shaped yellow flowers, male at first, then both male and female, hide under the leaves. Six plants would probably be enough, but we always set in at least twice that many, which will easily produce a hundred dark green fruits with skins that are prickly when they first come off the vines. Then it's time to make cucumber, onion, tomato, and vinegar salad, time to make canned or frozen pickles, and time to find good homes for the fruits we cannot use. In the flush days of summer even the UPS driver takes away cucumbers.

No one takes away our winter squashes, no matter how abundant the yield of the vines. Even when the crop is generous, we're stingy, keeping almost every last butternut that the plants produce. Like cucumbers, melons, and summer squashes, winter squashes belong to the gourd family; the botanic designation for most of them, no matter the variety, is *Cucurbita maxima,* the "greatest gourd." And though all have flesh that ranges from yellow to golden orange, the varieties are legion: the gourd-shaped butternuts that always grace our garden; the plump little acorns with ridged black or dark green shells; the buttercups, sometimes called turbans because their contours suggest that headdress worn in southern Asia; the stout, elongated banana squashes that can weigh in at a hefty ten to thirty pounds; the equally huge, rounded Hubbards with warty blue skin; and some of the biggest types of pumpkins. (Some pumpkins, hard shelled though they be, are considered *C. pepo,* the "marrow gourd," which is the species to which the otherwise bland summer squashes belong.) The kind we grow, the butternuts, are neither marrow gourd nor greatest gourd but rather *C. moschata,* the "musky gourd." People who have traced the origins of plants generally agree that most squashes, especially the winter varieties, including pumpkins, originated in the New World and were domesticated for raising as food crops some nine thousand years before the first Europeans arrived. When the Pilgrims landed here, it was Indians who introduced them to winter squashes. Several decades earlier, in the late 1500s, Thomas Harriott listed *Macóqwer*—"called by us, *Pompions, Mellions,* and *Gourdes,* because they are of the like formes as those kindes in England"—as one of the truly tasty foods raised by the Native inhabitants. Harriott implies that some members of the gourd family had already made their way to England by the time he first saw and reported on *Macóqwer,* and in the early part of the seventeenth century John Gerard suggests the same thing, for he describes eight kinds of "Pompion," both cultivated and wild. He identifies one of them as "the Virginian Macocke," a word that is a variant of *Macóqwer.* There are indeed members of the gourd family—melons among them—that are indigenous to the Old World, but the delicious New World pumpkins and squashes crossed the ocean almost instantly once the first European adventurers had discovered these choice edibles in the early sixteenth century. I know their delight at the taste. Perhaps, as Native Americans have long done (and do to this day), they also delighted in the golden squash blossoms that grow as big around as a salad plate. The hairy, square-stemmed vines spill luxuriantly out of the hills in which the seeds were planted, and as with cucumbers, the pollinating male blossoms develop first and are later joined by female flowers. In mid-July I start looking under the large, slightly prickly leaves. In the beginning the butternut fruit is a faintly greenish white, pale as a grub, but when it's ripe the skin becomes tan and the meat, a glowing orange gold. Unlike cucumbers and the summer squashes, which must be eaten before reaching hard-seeded maturity, the butternuts and their close kin attain their full glory when the seeds are fully formed. They also store exceedingly well: Placed in a basket or a cardboard box, they'll last all winter. And oh, they are nutritious, containing more carbohydrates, fat, protein, and vitamin A than any of the summer squashes. We bake them, puree and freeze them, add them to the dough of sweet breads, use them instead of pumpkin in a pie.

Nor is that the end of what we grow. The other vegetable that always inhabits our garden is the bean—green string beans, yellow wax beans, and bush or pole lima beans. They loom so large in the ground, at our table, and in our lives that they deserve a chapter to themselves.

FULL OF BEANS

JUNE 14: THE WAX BEANS BECKON. The seeds were planted on April 25, when the moon was growing toward the full. As usual, I failed to sow them in a straight line, and the plants popped up like a miniature serpentine wall, curving this way, then that. Now fruits, banana yellow and as big around as my little finger, hang abundant amid the heart-shaped green leaves. The temperature outside reads ninety degrees, with a wringing wet share of humidity. I fold a bandanna into a sweatband, tie it around my head, and grab a tea towel to wipe the drips and runnels that the band can't catch. Then it's out to the bean patch with a five-gallon bucket and the three-legged aluminum and canvas stool that the Chief has dubbed my "sit-upon." The aging back finds it easier to alternate standing with sitting.

We have courted this moment. But picking beans is tedious work. It's stoop labor. Lift the leaves, inspect one side of the plant, pluck off the pods. The first beans hit the bottom of the bucket with a soft clatter. Bend plant, inspect its other side, pick again, and move on to the next batch of beans. We've put in double rows of both green and wax string beans—that is, two rows of each variety,

set side by side and only eight inches apart, and they're all fifty feet long. No, as long as eternity. Bend, pick, move, and bend again. I use the tea towel to wipe away the sweat that trickles down from under my eyes and the hairline at the back of my neck.

But the effort bears a sure reward, of course—beans steadily filling the bucket. Their yellow color creates a lambent glow. And thank goodness, these are snap beans, not string beans. *String bean* is, to be sure, a generic term for both the green and yellow varieties, so called for the tough filament that holds one side of the pod to the other. But the strings in the beans that we grow were selectively bred out of them in the nineteenth century.

Bend, pick, and move. Other small events ease the tedium. For one, there's music: A mockingbird in the New Field hedgerow gives a splendid concert that incorporates the cheery aria of a Carolina wren, the *pity-trp-trp* call of the rose-red summer tanager, the rattle of a belted kingfisher, and the whippoorwill-like song of the chuck-will's-widow that haunts the Point's summer nights. Nearby a pine warbler trills, an indigo bunting sings its sweetly lisping couplets. There's also sheer noise: the short, dry cough of a fish crow and that goldurned rooster cockadoodling. The Chief has taken to calling him Cockadoodle-Stew for the method of silencing that he'd like to take but won't. There's action in the garden, too: A small contingent of the mallards from the drainage pond on the other side of the hedgerow waddles into Garden Field and grazes as I pick. Something spooks them, and, raising a ruckus of quacks, they lift into the air. A cotton-tail rabbit dashes out of the bean row six feet ahead and leaps toward the hedgerow; a few beans six feet along will show the marks of its busy teeth. The bean plants themselves are alive with motion—little grasshoppers as green as the foliage, hopping crickets, and at least a thousand strutting, scurrying daddy longlegs. Luckily, bean-devouring beetles are few this year; those that I do find, I lovingly pinch between finger and thumb.

Then—oh, serendipity! Two feet from the end of the wax beans' double row, a pattern—a domed tessellation of black and burnt orange—appears in the cave of moist dark green shade beneath the leaves. Box turtle! A terrestrial creature, a reptile, but I'm as excited as if I'd discovered a gnome. I lift it gently from its resting place. Red eyes and slightly concave plastron—it's male. A female's plastron would be straight, her eyes brown or yellow. Back beneath the leaves he goes.

Though you can't predict the appearance of a turtle any more than you can predict the goodwill of the garden's tutelary spirits, it's not truly uncommon to find one amid the beans. Eastern box turtles are indeed great fanciers of gardens. All the nourishment a turtle needs is there, from meat to vegetables: earthworms, caterpillars, slugs, the blackberries running rampant from the site of a former mulch pile, the cucumbers and cantaloupes ripening on our vines. The great beaked mouth makes short work of soft food, but lack of teeth makes chewing impossible. This particular box turtle has taken shelter beneath the leaves not just for a chomp or three on my beans but also for the condition of the earth. We've had three weeks of drought. The garden has been watered, however, and the turtle, sensibly seeking relief from heat and dryness, has homed in on a cool, damp place.

His formal name is *Terrapene carolina,* "Carolina terrapin," though his species is hardly restricted to the Carolinas. The word *terrapin* comes from the family of Algonquian languages spoken by Indians who occupied territory from the coast to the plains beyond the Appalachians in eastern North America. The box turtle has long inhabited the wooded places all over the Algonquians' range and may be found in Mexico as well. It has a western counterpart—*T. ornata,* the "ornamented terrapin," a flat-shelled species that lives in open places on the Central Plains. Both are remarkable feats of anatomical engineering. They can shut their shells so tightly, hinged plastron closing firm against carapace, that a knife cannot be inserted, and a locked-up shell can support two hundred times its owner's weight. The two-pound turtle that I've found could bear my weight without being crushed, indeed without being hurt at all. Box turtles, like all turtles, have a keen sense of smell and can see the world in color—yellow, green, blue, and red. (In theory, then, the gnome beneath my beans can tell the difference between the wax variety and the green; I suspect, however, that odor is the determining factor—color be damned, it's the smell of a bean that identifies it as food.) And if they survive the various perils of turtlehood—a traffic accident when giant car runs over tiny tank as it trudges all unaware across a road, or malnutrition at the hands of someone who picks up and takes home a wild, free pet—then they might well live for more than ten decades. One record of longevity amazes me: A marked eastern box turtle attained the venerable age of 138 years. Oh, turtle in the beans, be safe.

The picking is finished; the five-gallon bucket's half full. But work has not yet come to an end. Thanks be that the next task, stemming and snapping, may be done sitting down. I wash the trimmed beans, pack them into canning jars, and turn on the stove. Forty minutes in the pressure canner and they're done, eight pints of sunshine for the dark weeks of winter.

This marks the beginning. The green beans—bush string beans of the 'Blue Lake' variety—come in four days after the wax beans.

Every day, then, fair weather or foul, I head for the bean patch, sweatband around head, sit-upon slung over shoulder, and bucket in hand. Some years the plants are so productive that I'll make nine pickings of each variety. Other years the supply is exhausted after only three excursions down the rows. Nonetheless, each of the three may have yielded a full bucket and more, while the nine may have brought less than half a bucket per picking. The difference lies partly in the weather, partly in the extent to which weeding and tilling have defeated the vegetation that always intrudes.

As I pick, stem, snap, and can—and wait for the pole limas to produce, an event that won't occur till the third week in August—beans obsess me. Daylong I talk beans, think beans, cook and eat beans. At night I dream beans. Lift, pick, bend, move on. The rhythms temper both wakeful hours and REM sleep. My whole body runs with sweat, I wipe my forehead with a rainbow of bandannas, and the slim green and yellow rods clatter endlessly into buckets. It is the experience that Robert Frost recounted when he wrote of harvesting apples and the dreams that possess him afterward—the colors and shapes of apples, the ache impressed on his instep by standing on a ladder rung, the rumble of apples rolling into the cellar bin: "For I have had too much / Of apple-picking: I am overtired / Of the great harvest I myself desired."

Yet I look at the growing accumulation of beans in Mason jars and grin. There's been another sort of harvest, too: a growing store of bean trivia, some of it serious, some silly. Blame it on restless curiosity, which is the sort that wants to know the names of living things so that they may be regarded as acquaintances, not as anonymous—and therefore suspect—strangers.

Bean—the word itself is bumptious and shows up in many guises: full of beans, not worth a bean, a bean counter, a string bean of a man. It comes to us straight from the curt Teutonic side of English—the Germans say *Bohne,* a close cognate—though not until after the Spanish explorers came traipsing through the New World (sometimes in full suits of armor) was the type of bean that I pick transported to Europe and the word *bean* applied to it. These beans are native to Central and South America. The name bestowed on them by science is *Phaseolus vulgaris;* the first part is classical Greek for "bean," and the second, Latin for "common."

The prime European bean, a member of the same family, is *Vicia faba,* the broad, or fava, bean. It's indigenous to northern Africa and southwestern Asia but widely and anciently naturalized elsewhere, particularly on the shores of the Mediterranean. In ancient Egypt broad beans by the ton were offered to the gods of the Nile, and their hollow stems were believed to facilitate the passage of souls to the land of the dead. The binomial means "vetch bean"—*faba* being Latin for "bean." And modern classificatory science has chosen *faba* as the basis for the name of an entire order of plants, the Fabales, which includes not just beans and their close cousins the peas but also mimosas and acacias, peanuts, clover, and kudzu. Most Fabales, including green, wax, and broad beans, have developed a win-win symbiosis with nitrogen-fixing bacteria, which live amid their roots and help convert the air's otherwise unusable nitrogen into soluble nitrates; the plants in turn leave nitrates in the soil—a valuable resource for both wild plants and those that are cultivated.

In modern Italian the *b* of the Latin *faba* has softened to *v*—*fava.* And there's a French version of the word for the broad bean—*fève;*

in that land, however, *P. vulgaris,* the New World green beans that command my dreams, are known as *haricots verts.* This variety of bean, beloved in France and specially bred to be slim, is picked when its pods are six or so inches long but less than an eighth of an inch in diameter. *Haricot*—the term struck my ear as distinctive, eccentric even, until I learned that it is a transmutation of the Aztec word *ayecott.* That makes sense—the come-lately term points to the bean's ancient place of origin. It has also produced a most peculiar off-shoot: The name of zydeco, a dance music favored in southern Louisiana, is an elision, Cajun style, of *les haricots,* "the beans." Spanish has also gone off on a tack of its own, referring to beans in general as *judia* or *habichuela,* though anyone who patronizes Taco Bell will eat the red beans called frijoles.

I've found broad beans, bagged in plastic and labeled ITALIAN BEANS, amid the frozen vegetables at the supermarket. The pods are wide and flat compared to those of the slender but round six-inch beans that I've been picking. The taste, however, is equally redolent of earth and sun. Nevertheless, broad beans have immemorially been implicated in a most unpleasant hereditary allergy called favism. William Woys Weaver, master gardener and contemporary writer on heirloom vegetable gardening, maintains that the modern fava is not the same as the bean cooked in ancient Mediterranean kitchens; that the bean we eat today is of another variety from that found by archaeologists in old hearths and middens. "Carbonized favas from Roman sites," says Weaver, "prove that the seeds were small, like peas; some were even the size of lentils." He adds that the large broad beans did not appear until the ninth century. But the significant word here is *variety.* The ancient and modern beans are not separate entities but rather variations on the theme of *V. faba,* and both may bring on favism in those who are vulnerable.

The polymath Pythagoras (c. 580–500 B.C.), a Greek who lived in the south of Italy, is surely best known to day for his famous theorem about the sum of the squares of the legs of a right triangle equaling the square of the hypotenuse. He also passed on the belief of his Egyptian teachers, with whom he studied for twelve years, that the souls of the dead are given passage to the hereafter by the broad bean. He is credited, moreover, with issuing a stern warning to his compatriots in southern Italy: Do not eat broad beans. Pliny, who knew for certain that beans were magical, echoes Pythagoras's warning, saying that the Greeks banned eating them because they dulled the senses and caused insomnia. Beans represented a type of grain to Pliny, and he honored them for their many practical uses: They could be served up plain at the table, mixed with other grains and used as flour for bread, or stewed as an offering to the gods. Beyond that, they were allied with the forces of heaven, for they contained the souls of the dead and brought luck to those who carried a bean home from the harvest. Pythagoras was right. Broad beans can indeed trigger trouble. Primarily afflicting men, particularly those of Mediterranean descent, the allergy brings on fever, jaundice, and hemolytic anemia, a type of anemia that blasts the body's red blood cells to kingdom come. It can be fatal. Still, science has recently discovered a boon conferred by inheriting the gene that causes favism. Those at risk, those who should always shun broad beans, have inherited two copies of the mutant gene that causes favism, one from the mother, one from the father. But in individuals who carry only a single copy, the gene acts to protect them from malaria. The mutation, like the genes that lead to sickle-cell anemia and cystic fibrosis, arose as a defense against disease.

Beans are said to be dangerous in another way:

> Beans, beans, the musical fruit—
> The more you eat, the more you toot.
> The more you eat, the better you feel.
> So eat your beans at every meal.

That's the euphemistic version of a ditty that my children brought home from junior high school (shades of the campfire scene in Mel Brooks's *Blazing Saddles*). The more rambunctious, less polite version begins, "Beans, beans, they're good for your heart." Beans have long been blamed for postprandial flatulence. The 1633 edition of Gerard's *Herball* contains vigorous woodcuts portraying eleven kinds of Old and New World beans, along with the seeds of some; whatever the variety, each plant is shown winding around a pole, reaching energetically toward heaven. Speaking of broad beans, Gerard has this to say about The Problem: "The Beane is windie meate. And seeing the meate of Beans is windie, the Beans themselves if they be boyled whole and eaten are yet much more windie. If they be parched they lose their windiness, but they are harder of digestion." But Gerard absolves "Kidney Beanes," the name that both he and present-day Englishmen use for green, wax, and other *Phaseolus* species because the beans resemble that organ. He says: "The fruits and cods of Kidney Beanes boiled together before they be ripe, and buttered, and so eaten with their cods are exceedingly delicate meat, and do not ingender winde as the other Pulses do." What a peculiar surprise! I understand at last what I've known all along, that we eat beans and many other vegetables before they're ripe. "Ripe" has to do with setting seeds, with the future of the species, and Gerard characterizes the fully mature stage of beans as "neither toothsome nor wholesome."

To begin with, green beans and many other vegetables, like limas and eggplants, must be cooked before they're eaten. Raw beans contain powerful antienzymes, substances that hinder digestion by binding to other nutrients, like proteins, or to enzymes in the alimentary tract—lo, the goodness of beans passes right through instead of being absorbed. But cooking breaks down antienzymes and allows the body to make use of the nourishment in the vegetable. Long before humankind loomed on the horizon, plants developed antienzymes and toxins as defenses against being eaten before they could reproduce. Since people settled down and started to farm, selective breeding has reduced the antienzymes and toxins found in food plants. (I'm safe, then, nibbling lustily on raw beans as I pick: There's something delicious about a tender young pod.) As for the windiness that's engendered by eating beans, modern science has found its cause. With dried beans, flatulence is produced by the indigestible starches, stachyose and raffinose, that they contain. In the case of fresh beans sugars are the culprits; they are not broken down by digestive enzymes in the upper intestine—antienzymes are at work—but when they reach the lower regions, bacteria degrade them and in the process produce gas. The classic remedy for avoiding The Problem when eating baked beans, seven-bean soup, confetti green beans, or other bean dishes is to accompany the meal with applesauce (to me a far more appealing choice than the commercial preparation called Beano).

And still no end to beans, no end to labor. No end, either, to the mockingbird's concerts, the rooster's lusty, near-constant crowing, and the creatures found amid the leaves—a tiny southern cricket frog with skin of mottled beige and brown, and several rosy wolf-snails. The latter, native to the New World's steamy South, are car-nivores and, because of their meat-eating ways, were taken to Hawaii in 1955 to combat another introduced species, the giant African snail, which has a most unseemly appetite for crops. But the wolfsnail soon gave up pursuit of its intended prey and began to feast on *Achatinella,* a large genus of snails indigenous to Oahu. The upshot: Fifteen to twenty native species of the genus are gone for-ever, with the remaining members now on the endangered list. What the wolfsnail eats here, I do not know, but its presence, kept in check by long-ago-instated natural controls, threatens nothing. Conical shell of dusty rose red—I find it beautiful to look at. Then, on the seventh picking, serendipity again appears suddenly, quietly out of nowhere: Beneath the leaves is the tiniest box turtle that I've ever seen. Its domed carapace is no bigger around than a silver dollar. The size indicates a real youngster, a hatchling from this very year. I pick it up—female, and her pudgy little clawed feet never once stop scrabbling to get away. As soon as she hits the ground again, she runs. The hare would have a hard time keeping up with her.

Seven pickings, sixty-three pints canned and frozen—that's more than a year's supply for the Chief and me. Some will be given away, gifts from both of us, for the Chief helps with the canning—timing, removing jars, putting the canner away till the next time. (He also watches me ardently as I stem and snap; his excuse is that someone has to supervise me lest I start—as I sometimes do—putting the stems in with the beans.) We may be through with beans, but beans aren't through with us—they still produce with prodigious abun-dance. So I offer them to our neighbor Becky for the picking, and when she arrives, five-gallon bucket in hand, I grab a bucket, too, and work down the double row of yellow beans while she harvests the green. A picking bee—it's certainly the easiest way to make light of hard labor. We talk without cease. She and her husband, Dennis, are vegetable gardeners on a grand scale and have just dug and canned more than a hundred quarts of their own red potatoes—and that's only half the crop. I delight in visiting their place—garden after garden featuring such delights as scarlet runner beans, a forest of asparagus, wildflowers, a weed relocation project, and homemade outsider art. They keep chickens, too, but their cock, a Rhode Island Red named Leonard, manages to practice admirable restraint when it comes to crowing. Becky takes home a five-gallon bucket brimming with slender green-and-yellow glory.

And sure as sunrise, there will be more beans—beans for other neighbors, beans for our supper table, beans for drying. I find myself looking forward to the two-month hiatus between the final harvest of these ground-hugging bush plants and the ripening of the pole limas. The only task left is to leave the few beans still forming to dry on the bushes; the pods will be harvested when they are brown, and the seeds—pure white for the green beans, and for the yellow, white with a dash of purple at the point of attachment to the pod—will be shelled out and saved for making soup. Meanwhile the tomatoes will need attention, and the eggplants, cucumbers, and winter squashes. The river will also summon me to set the gill net and at least seven crab pots to be fished every other day. We need a winter's supply of seafood, too.

But when the limas begin to come in toward the end of August, it's as if no time at all has passed. The picking, however, is far less hard on legs and back, for I harvest this crop standing up, with an occasional stoop to get the pods hanging close to the ground.

Climbing beans will race up anything that's handy, from the nearest tree to the high-dollar towers and the A-frames of metal strung with nylon cord that are sold in the seed catalogs. But the Chief has built a fence for our pole beans, setting several stout four-by-fours in the ground and stretching five-foot-high wire fencing from one post to the next. It's a permanent installation; the beans should fling themselves around and up it right merrily for years to come. The row itself is thirty feet long. In the past we've planted the small baby 'Fordhooks,' a bush type; sometimes we've reaped a good harvest, sometimes the weeds overwhelmed the crop. It takes limas a full three months, far longer than the snap beans, to reach the picking stage. So the weeds have more time to insinuate themselves, and in the sultry heat of summer I'm not always inclined to leave the air-conditioned trailer to yank out the upstarts that rear their stems, leaves, and tendrils high above the bush limas. Now, for two good reasons, we've decided to try pole limas of the sort that country people call "potato beans" because they're rounded and meaty. One is to give the beans a fighting chance to rise above their brash green competitors. The other is that I've missed the fun of picking pole beans. Time was, during my first decade at the Point, I could steal the pole beans known as speckled butterbeans from Ebbie, one of our part-time neighbors, who'd come from town to his riverside place only as the garden behind his trailer needed tending. It was a huge garden, almost worthy of being called a farm. Okra, black-eyed and field peas, tomatoes, summer squashes, and two types of pole beans, a snap variety with purple pods and the speckled butterbeans—he grew southern specialties. Knowing full well that I'd head for Ebbie's garden when I went birding during the bean season, I'd tote not only my binoculars and sit-upon but also a bread bag for the sweet loot. Once a blue grosbeak nested in one of his okra plants; I spotted the nest as I was helping myself to supper from his vines. He couldn't have missed the beans I took, for he always planted enough to feed all of eastern North Carolina—three tall rows, and each at least a hundred feet long. The beans were of an immensely colorful sort that you don't often see these days—limas with purple splashes and speckles on their light gray skins. Cooked, they turn entirely gray. Where Ebbie got his seeds, I do not know; I think he must have saved some year to year from his own crop. The seeds of old-fashioned bean varieties are sometime available at local cooperative farm bureaus; another, surer source is seed companies that specialize in heirlooms. But for the last five years there've been no beans for me to steal. Age and infirmity have overtaken Ebbie. His garden lies fallow; nothing grows there but grass, which he occasionally drives out from town to mow.

Limas—pure bliss! Be they sedate bush types or exuberant pole lovers, these beans are formally known as *Phaseolus limensis,* member of the same genus as our green and wax snap beans. The species name, "from Lima," indicates their origin in Peru, where their cultivation and use date back to at least 5000 B.C. Back in the 1600s John Gerard acknowledged their connection with the New World by calling the species the "Brasile Kidney Beane." His *Herball* illustrates it with woodcuts not only of the climbing vine but also of the plumped-out seedpod "in his ful bignesse." The picture of the pod shows a truly awe-inspiring lima with seeds as big as slightly elongated quarters. And the other limas shown are bright or as bold in pattern as Ebbie's speckled butterbeans: "seeds of divers colours; sometimes they are red, otherwhiles of a whitish colour, sometimes wholly black, and otherwhiles spotted." Thomas Jefferson also mightily admired limas. He was a bean man, anyhow, and in the highest degree. For decades, from the days of the Revolutionary War to 1824, his garden books show his true devotion to the fruit. And oh, the varieties that he grew: limas, fava beans of several types, and snap beans with a wild array of names—Bess beans, arbor beans, asparagus beans, slender red haricots, long haricots, marsh beans, dwarf beans of Holland, beans of Switzerland, wild goose beans, and a dozen others. Some catalogs advertise asparagus beans today; the pods are fourteen to thirty inches long. But the lima may well have been Jefferson's favorite, for his letters record that he often gave the seeds—along with the seeds of other more majestic greenery like oak, catalpa, and pecan trees—as gifts to friends in the States and in France.

As I pick the first limas—a mere handful, but enough for supper—I think of Jefferson and his Virginia home, Monticello, only forty miles over the Blue Ridge from where we winter. And I wonder if he—or more likely a field-hand slave—was watched from deep within the vines while picking pole beans. As I move along the row, my movements are observed. Every pole bean patch in the South must host a rough green snake, and this one is no exception. The little reptile's formal name is *Opheodrys aestivus*, "summer wood-land-snake," and it's found amid pole beans, thickets, woods, and elsewhere throughout the Carolinas and in Virginia, except for the Appalachians in the northwest portion of the last. A close cousin, *O. vernalis*, the smooth green snake or "spring woodland-snake," lives in those very mountains. The difference between smooth and rough is that the dorsal scales of *O. aestivus* are keeled, while the cousin's are flat. As snakes go, this species is small, with a two-foot-long body that's no bigger around than a clothesline. Its back is exactly the color of a tender new leaf, and its belly, a soft lemony yellow. Though the creature may gape if it's caught, and show the black interior of its mouth, it's not likely to bite. I spy it often as I harvest the tomatoes—'Roma' and 'Whopper'—that grow in the pole bean patch. Tongue flicking, head moving to follow my movements, it watches me from one or another leafy perch near the top of the five-foot fence. Pole limas are the link between us. They provide us both with food: the Chief and me with plump beans, the green snake with a well-stocked larder of vine-loving grasshoppers, crickets, spiders, and larval insects. We do not tell people that the vines are inhabited by a snake, for the name alone is enough to trigger the shudder factor. But there's nothing rough about a green snake except for its scales.

But at the end of August, right at the time that New Field should start producing limas in abundance, I flee the coast. The trunk and backseat of my car are filled with coolers bearing a summer's worth of bounty from the land and from the river: ten cubic feet of frozen broccoli, cauliflower, stewed tomatoes, cucumber pickles, crabmeat, and shrimp. Leaving the Chief behind (he's a stubborn man), I depart in darkness and frog-drowning rain. Hurricane Dennis has aimed its great fist at the coast. Inevitably, the electricity will go out. Aiming to save the work of many months, I head for Virginia and a freezer connected to a reliable source of power. On returning four days later I find the pole bean fence toppled, the great green vines sprawling on the earth like leafy pillows. The Chief reports that the river rose eight feet and breaking waves rolled into both gardens. When the earth has dried, I check the vines: another handful. Two weeks later another hurricane strikes. We both flee. Bridges are washed out, great trees lie across the roads, towns and cities are drowned by greasy brown high-water floods. Eleven days elapse before the roads are clear enough for our return. When we reach Great Neck Point, the eggplants and bell peppers have somehow risen from the salt and are bearing miraculous fruit, but the vines have died; the poles and fence lie on the ground. We'll try again next year.

Meanwhile the green and wax beans are safe. We'll eat them, along with the garden's other gifts—and be suffused not only with flavor but also with memories of hot southern sun, of ancient bean lore, and—best—of the many lives that share the bean patch with us.

PARSLEY, SAGE, ROSEMARY, AND LEMON THYME

THE HERB GARDEN IS AN ACCIDENT. I'd never intended to grow the classic seasonings. If we needed basil, say, or parsley, I'd visit a neighbor who grew it and ask for a leaf or a bunch. But herbs arrived in our yard anyhow, and piecemeal, in small, recycled green plastic pots that may once have held tomato seedlings, baby jalapeños, sedums, or marigolds. They arrived because of the birds.

Great Neck Point lies on the great Atlantic Flyway. It rests at an intersection of north and south. The result: birds, birds, and more birds. I've tallied more than 220 species in our neighborhood, in its yards, fields, and woods and over the river. Three different flocks of birders make regular spring and fall visits to our place; we walk the roads and lanes, the paths through the woods, and along the river-shore to see what we can see. Not only the sights but also the sounds are grand: the ear-piercing *PEET-sup* of an otherwise unobtrusive Acadian flycatcher, the blue-gray gnatcatcher's whispered complaints, the nasal *haaah-haaah* of a laughing gull, the sewing machine rattle of a belted kingfisher as it stitches the river to its banks. The birders bring snacks for the trail and lunches, complete with homemade

fudge and brownies, to devour at the picnic tables near water's edge in the front yard. They also bring gifts—note cards, banana bread, plants. And that's how herbs came into my life.

It was Barbara, from the crossroads community of Arapahoe on the other side of the river, who started the garden. She bore a four-inch-tall sprig of rosemary, newly rooted in one of those ubiquitous green plastic pots. I put it in the earth forthwith. Several months later, on a misty, moist Sunday, Barbara boarded the ferry and made a special, nonbirding trip across the river to bring me more plants, some of them purely decorative. They included dill, chives, lemon thyme, Queen Anne's lace, and pennyroyal. Observing gardener's manners, I did not thank her, for thanking the donor of a plant is said to bring on blight and worms at best, and at worst an instant drooping unto death. The dill, an annual, was used within the month for making pickles. When the date for northward migration came, I covered the bed with pine straw and hoped that some, if not all, would survive the winter's rigors.

The rosemary and chives did, and the Queen Anne's lace as well, though only for a year. But that short sprig of rosemary insisted on life. When we made a January foray to the river, the chives were dormant but the rosemary stood in its bed, rising above the winter mulch like a miniature pine tree, no taller than it had been when it came to Great Neck Point but just as green, just as resinous in scent, just as proudly upright as it had been on the day that it entered my life. Late that spring it began to branch. That summer it became clear that the rosemary was headed toward shrubdom and would soon outgrow its bed. I moved it to a new location near Sally Doberdog's grave at the west end of the garden in Garden Field. And there it flourished, becoming a bush, a giant bush eight feet around, and its topmost branches now tickle my chin. (That's nothing: Rosemary growing in Tuscany may not infrequently reach a height of fifteen feet.) Blossoms blue as cornflowers deck the branches in spring and often in fall as well.

Rosmarinus officinalis—"edible dew of the sea"—has an ancient connection to humanity. This native of Mediterranean countries was once believed to be especially fond of growing in sight of the sea, though it's always had a foothold inland, too. It migrated early on to other countries; in his *Herball* John Gerard writes that it was used in Germany as a spice, in Languedoc as fuel for fire, and in Italy and England as an ornamental plant that makes a sturdy hedge, especially when set against a wall. It came to the New World with the first wave of colonization, of course. It has long served more than culinary, fire-making, and landscaping purposes; its virtues are manifold. Sir Thomas More (1478–1535) has this to say: "As for Rosmarine, I lett it runne all over my garden walls, not onlie because my bees love it, but because it is the herb sacred to remembrance, and, therefore, to friendship." Rosemary for remembrance, rosemary for friendship—that's not all. There's rosemary for faithfulness and sending away bad dreams, rosemary for Christmas decorations and flavoring wine, rosemary for keeping moths out of clothes presses, curing gout, and fending off bubonic plague, rosemary to signify that, where it thrives, a woman dominates the household. Once upon a time in England, rosemary bushes might be intentionally damaged to show that a man ruled the roost after all. Whole branchlets were cast into graves; burned, they served as incense and were used in hospitals to purify the air. And as it happens, rosemary and most commonly used culinary herbs and spices, along with onions and garlic, have potent antibacterial and antifungal properties; they are capable of killing or, at least, slowing down the microorganisms that often taint and spoil food. Thomas Jefferson, however, employed rosemary for its flavor and grew it in his Monticello garden in the company of other herbs like sage, thyme, chives, marjoram, and two varieties of parsley. Rosemary's truest virtue—as Jefferson surely believed, along with me and a salivating multitude of others—is its compatibility with food: lamb, chicken, potatoes, and herb breads.

A forest of rosemary now overshadows the chives and lemon thyme. High time to transplant both to a place in the sun. Officially, chives are called *Allium schoenoprasum,* "rush-leek onion," for their taste and their slender leaves. Till Barbara brought me the tame variety, I was happily using the wild onion grass that sprouts willy-nilly and well-nigh ineradicably in fields and gardens alike. That ubiquitous stuff imbued milk with its strong flavor when the cows were turned out to pasture in spring at Justamere Farm—ugh! Luckily, onion grass died back with the onset of summer, and the milk would be sweet again. Science knows onion grass as *A. stellatum,* "starry onion," perhaps for its burst of starlike pale purple blooms. Apart from its evil effect on milk, it serves nobly—though not quite so potently as chives—to gussy up potato salad or mix with sour cream for topping baked potatoes; washed and chopped, it freezes well enough to ensure a winter's supply. And the little wild bulbs, no bigger around than large peas, are sweet when boiled and served up with butter.

Lemon thyme is the most persistently modest plant I've ever known. It hugs the earth like a thin green table mat and quietly trails out its stems and leaves, diminutive leaves, each no bigger around than the eye of a fruit fly. And by the time the rosemary overshadowed it, the plant had attained a full foot and a half in diameter.

Weeding around the mat of lemon thyme, rooting an impertinent stalk of wild lettuce right out of its center, I break off a few leaves and rub them between my fingers: The citrus smell is as tart and fresh as that of its namesake, and so is the flavor. I recall an image drawn by the Roman poet Virgil (70–19 B.C.) in his *Georgics,* those elegant hexameters on aspects of farming: Young bees flying back to the hive in the evening, their legs laden with pollen from the thyme flowers they had visited daylong. Thyme honey was famous in the ancient world. Virgil's Mediterranean was also the original home of *Thymus vulgaris,* or "common thyme." The lemon thyme that so pleases my nose and taste buds is *T.* x *citriodorus,* "lemon-scented," a hybrid derived from *T. serpyllum,* the wild thyme that attracted the foraging bees on ancient hillsides. *T. serpyllum* combines Greek and Latin words for the same things and translates as "thyme thyme."

After Barbara has presented her grand potpourri of herbal offerings, the other birders begin bringing in their own contributions: one pot of sage to begin with, then another, and one of winter savory, one of parsley. The birding on parsley day is better than hoped for. The songs of migrating warblers sizzle and ring in the woods: the lisp of a northern parula, the delicate ascending trill of a prairie warbler, the tuneful *wee-weechy* of a common yellowthroat, the ovenbird's almost earsplitting shout, and the yellow-throated warbler's melodious *sweet-sweet-I'm-so-sweet.* The music makes us rich.

The day after the parsley arrives I transplant it into the large, earth-filled Styrofoam box that sits on the back deck. And behold: Along comes the High Cockalorum! I've known her slightly for the year that she and her family have lived at the Point, but only over the parsley do I recognize her at last for what she is. A cockalorum is usually thought of as male, a little man given to self-importance. But this one is female, a woman fully grown though slight in frame. I've had little to do with her. So it took me a whole year—the year that she's lived among us at the Point—to recognize her as a true example of the self-preening kind. She lives in the house next door to that of the owner of the ever-cockadoodling rooster, but I swear that she, in her own mild-voiced way, can outcrow him. And on this day, she has been strutting around to see what she can see. "Hi," I say, "how're you doing?" She watches for a moment, then says, "Ugly planter."

So I tell her the story of how it came to be a planter. My elder son and his rose-growing wife found it while beachcombing a mile or so upriver. There it sat on the sand, a white Styrofoam container a yard long and a foot wide with blue lettering on one end: CAPTAIN SEA BRAND, a container for crabmeat. Below the label are little boxes in which the kind of crabmeat—lump, backfin, special—could be checked off. I imagine it came from one of the crab-picking establishments that cluster on this rivershore. But there it was beached, marooned, a castaway, an orphan. What else could they do but bring it home? As soon as I saw it, I knew that it deserved another life as a box to hold plants. With a screwdriver, small holes were punched through near the bottom so that water can drain out. It was then filled with a mixture of mulch, potting soil, and earth from the plot in Garden Field. In its first season it held tall, frilly orange marigolds. This year it's destined as a home for some of the more tender herbs. The first of them is parsley, which blooms one year, then bolts and dies the next.

"Hmm," says the Cockalorum. "I wouldn't have anything like that at my house."

But it works, the planter works. Basil was put in, along with the parsley—and that occasioned another comment from the High

Cockalorum, who came by early one morning as I was snipping off strong-scented green leaves for chopping and putting into the freezer, but I'll come to that shortly. The basil, an annual, is long gone, except for what's been frozen or dried, but the parsley still thrives in the box that once held Captain's Choice Crab—not the original plant but its children, for I let it go to seed after several ounces of its leaves had been dried and after it had nourished a summer's worth of black swallowtail caterpillars. *Petroselinum crispum,* its botanical name, means "closely curled rock-parsley." *Selinum,* Latin for "parsley," is formed from the Greek word *selinon;* the Greeks distinguished between two kinds of the stuff—mountain parsley and marsh parsley. The latter translates their term for celery, which requires much water for its growth, while the mountain type clearly favors higher, drier habitats. This parsley that I've planted is the latter. But its leaves aren't curled and ruffled; it's rather the plain, flat-leaved sort, the one preferred for cooking because it is more flavorful than —though not so pretty as—curly parsley. Native to the eastern Mediterranean area, the plant in all its guises is cultivated now around the world. Apparently, stone still provides a suitable habitat, at least in England and Scotland, to which it was introduced in the sixteenth century; there it quickly naturalized itself in rocky places and on old walls. But I do not give the Cockalorum any of these facts; nor is it likely that she'd be interested in a disquisition on the ways in which antiquity put parsley to work. Its uses back then were legion. Although people didn't eat it at first because it was sacred to the dead, Homeric heroes fed it to their horses. And at the Isthmian and Nemean games, two of the great athletic contests held in Greece, the winners' crowns were made of parsley woven into wreaths (the crowns at Delphi and Olympia were wrought of bay laurel and wild olive, respectively). That is all the material reward that a runner, boxer, or charioteer could expect from victory in the games: a green chaplet of fragrant leaves. It goes without saying, however, that glory was also showered on the victor, his family, and his community.

Parsley attracts black swallowtail butterflies as milk attracts cats. *Swallowtail*—the name refers to the delicate, tail-like projections on each hind wing. Summerlong, I see them fluttering one at a time above the leaves. Later I'll find the eggs, sparsely distributed, one on this leaf, two on that stem. But the plants usually produce enough food for both of us, woman and butterfly. So I tend to leave the eggs alone and watch as the larvae develop. On hatching they are each no bigger than a dark whisker; as they move from leaf to leaf, they munch, growing all the while into handsome caterpillars, sometimes called parsleyworms, that are green and black striped dappled with gold. And if you touch one, it will rear up, emitting a rank odor and sprouting a pair of soft orange horns from a Y-shaped gland in its head; action and smell are meant, of course, to rout a predator. In their ceaseless thrust toward metamorphosis they sometimes devour every bit of my parsley clean down to the roots. Nor is that all they eat; they'll go for carrot tops, too, and zero in on celery, dill, fennel, and other members of the parsley family. When they've had their fill, they creep away to form a chrysalis that will not release its sleeping contents until spring. But roots are all the plants need to resurrect themselves; almost overnight the box will fill again with lusty greenery. Again *Papilio polyxenes* will hover above the leaves, alight, and lay her eggs.

P. polyxenes—*papilio* is the Latin word for "butterfly." The species name, chosen by Linnaeus himself for reasons that have vanished into the maw of time, honors one of the doomed princes born to

Priam, king of Troy. Other members of the same genus also commemorate noble warriors: Glaucus, a Trojan ally who exchanged his golden armor for bronze, is remembered in the tiger swallowtail; the Trojan prince Troilus is recalled in the spicebush; and the palamedes is eponymous with the Greek Palamedes, who unveiled the wily Odysseus's ruse of madness to avoid military service.

Fierce names for such airy creatures! But as it happens, the male black swallowtail is an aggressive insect, with habits as black as its wings. It emerges from its chrysalis a few days earlier in spring than does the female. First come, first served: At once it begins to stake out territory, preferably atop a hill. Once there, it will try to fight off all other males that come flying in. It's been reported that a male caught fast in the butterfly equivalent of rut will try to drive off anything black, be it a red-winged blackbird or a black T-shirt. It's the midnight color that counts: This not only triggers the male's defense of his chosen mating ground but is also used by both sexes to deceive. Deception lies in the coloration of the wings—black, with two rows of golden spots along the edges and, in the female, dusted on the lower hind wing with iridescent blue. The bodies of some butterflies and their larvae contain noxious chemicals because of the food that they ingest—bitter, emetic milkweed for the monarch, poisonous Dutchman's-breeches for the pipevine swallowtail. Birds learn that lepidopterans like these can make them powerfully sick and learn, as well, to avoid them. The wings of the pipevine swallowtail are black; its perfectly palatable black swallowtail cousin mimics that protective coloration.

Both butterflies and bees love the oregano that lives and sprawls beside the rosemary forest. If I'm not quick enough to cut it back, it quietly explodes with clusters of small white blossoms up and down amid the leaves on woody stems as long as my forearm. And the insects come, dancing in the air, landing to sip nectar, rising to dance again. Apart from painted ladies and buckeyes I cannot identify the butterflies, except to think that they are skippers, for they are small and generally drab in color. But oh, the energy that they expend in their adoration of oregano! I'm of two minds, however, about *Origanum vulgare,* "common oregano," a perennial member of the mint family (some of the herbs that share its genus are annuals). Its habits are indeed vulgar; they're those of a weed. Install the plant and you'll find that it's almost immune to eradication. True weeds do not crowd it out, nor does the rosemary's heavy shade. It spreads with holier-than-thou persistence. On the other hand, this plant that's sometimes called wild marjoram serves my culinary purposes very well: Spaghetti sauce requires its robust flavor; stuffed eggplant fairly craves it. And I must admit that oregano's history is rich and honorable.

Origanum—the old Greek word means "mountain joy." In summer its superabundant blossoms gave a pink blush to the hillsides that it covered in its native Mediterranean habitat. The ancient Greeks believed that it had come into the world as a gift from Aphrodite, and when they married, couples might wear chaplets of the herb. Pliny mentions it as a necessary item in the Roman pharmacopoeia, as does his first-century A.D. contemporary Dioscorides, a Greek who served as a surgeon to the emperor Nero's troops and wrote extensively on the medical materials supplied by plants. In his glorious *Herball* Gerard calls it organy or bastard marjoram; he also cites the Spanish word *oregano,* which the New World has taken over wholesale. By his lights, the herb possesses a remarkable host of medicinal virtues: "Organy given in wine is a remedy against the bitings, and stingings of venomous beasts, and cureth them that have drunke *Opium.* It healeth scabs, itches, and scurvinesse, being used in baths, and it taketh away the bad colour which cometh of the yellow jaundice. The weight of a dram taken with meade or honied water, draweth forth by stool blacke and filthy humors, as *Dioscorides* and *Pliny* write." Perhaps the drug czars should emulate the pizza parlors and take a look at oregano's potency.

I've had little luck with its cousin sweet marjoram, *O. marjorana.* The species name, used of old, is a transformation of the Greek term *amarakos;* passing time has seen the dropping of the *a* and the softening of the *k* to *j.* But while I understand the changes in the word that designates the plant, I do not understand the plant itself. From seeds in starter pots to healthy seedlings in much larger clay pots, all went well at first. Water, Miracle-Gro, weeding, snipping off incipient blooms—the young marjoram was cherished. Perhaps too much so, for halfway through the summer it began to droop; the stems that should have developed some toughness went limp. Nothing, not water nor pleadings and imprecations, prevailed. The only course available was to cut the sad stems before they'd failed completely and put them in the dehydrator. So the effort was not without some small success: dried marjoram for herb butter, along with sage, savory, basil, and thyme.

Sage, savory, and thyme—it may be safe to thank the birders in print, where the plants can't hear me. The sage and winter savory, however, must be restarted, for the same back-to-back hurricanes that toppled the pole lima beans drowned them both, the sage in the earth by the shed, the savory in an elegant clay pot beside the steps to the back deck. The river rose out of its bed with wind-driven fury and rolled three feet deep, shoving water and strewing wreckage far into New Field and Garden Field. Is it ridiculous or oversentimental to mourn the deaths of plants? I do not feel the sorrow that struck— struck hard enough to keep me reeling for a year—at the death of

Sally Doberdog, but there is, nonetheless, a sense of loss. Where once there was savory with tiny soft-green leaves, where once there was silver-green sage, there is now only emptiness. A few leaves dried before the storms are all that remain.

Sage and winter savory: The first is *Salvia officinalis,* "useful healing-sage"; the latter, *Satureja montana,* "mountain savory," which is a perennial, unlike its genus mate *S. hortensis,* the half-hardy annual summer savory. Both originated in the Mediterranean—that cradle of herbs that has so generously provided the rest of the world with splendid seasonings. They were transported north and spread through western Europe by Roman troops. They took sail across the Atlantic, of course, with the very first colonists. Germans call winter savory *Bohnenkraut,* "bean plant," because it was often cooked along with beans and other legumes. It's not unlikely that savory was thought to combat The Bean Problem. Gerard vows that summer savory does just that: "It doth marvellously prevaile against winde: therefore it is with good successe boiled and eaten with beanes, peason, and other windie pulses." And sage, according to him, is even more miraculous, for it not only banishes flatulence but also strengthens memory, halts spontaneous abortions, banishes pleurisy, and, mixed with other herbs in wine, makes "an excellent water to wash the secret parts of man or woman." I miss these herbs. We'll try in the new year to raise them again.

The last two herbs that crown the garden are basil and bay, the latter not actually in the garden but on its outskirts. The bay is not the bay bought off the spice rack in the supermarket. The leaves packed in expensive little jars are those of *Laurus nobilis,* "noble laurel," better known as bay laurel. Originating in Anatolia and prehistorically naturalized throughout the Mediterranean, that bay figured in classical occasions: The Greeks set wreaths of bay laurel upon the heads of victors in the great Pythian games held at Delphi to honor Apollo; the Romans made laurel crowns for conquering generals and placed them also on their own noggins in celebration of the Saturnalia, a rowdy festival that lightened the dark, chilly depths of winter. Today the plant has ceased to deck pates but is reserved instead for culinary purposes and filling ornamental patio pots. Nonetheless, people are still said to have earned their laurels; nor is it uncommon for a city, state, or country to nominate a poet laureate. Our bay, native to the New World, is far more modest in habitat and history. It's called red bay or sweet bay and belongs, with its cousin *L. nobilis,* to the laurel family, which also includes such powerfully fragrant plants as cinnamon and sassafras. And red bay, just as aromatic and evergreen as its celebrated cousin, grows wild— free, that is, for the picking—in the hedgerows and ditch banks of coastal Carolina. Science dubs it *Persea borbonia,* "Bourbon's avocado." And it belongs indeed to the same genus as the avocado, while its species name honors Gaston de Bourbon, a seventeenth-century patron of botany and son of Henry IV of France. The plant, a mere shrub in our hedgerows, is actually a tree that can attain a height of sixty feet; its heavy, hard, bright red wood, described by one early writer on the New World's natural history as resembling "watered satin," is prized for cabinetmaking. Ah, red bay! I may never see a specimen big enough to warrant the lofty title of *tree,* but when I'm of a mind to cook up chili or a hearty soup, I go outside for a leaf or three to add to the steaming pot, where heat soon releases the plant's essential oils. And we dry leaves to take north each winter. No reason either that it shouldn't become a wreath. Slender, leafy branches twisted into a circle and hung with red ribbon upon a downstairs wall in our northern home would add a clean, crisp, summer-sweet aroma to the air.

My favorite herb, bar none, is basil. It comes in many incarnations. Plants may be dwarfs or giants, with leaves that range from minuscule to huge enough to wrap an entire chicken breast. The scents run the gamut from lemon and cinnamon to licorice and something I think of as pure spice-green. And the leaves may be glowing green, rich royal purple, or variegated, with amethyst here, emerald there. The variety that I usually plant is Italian large leaved. I start it in small pots, and when its secondary leaves begin to double their size overnight, I set the seedlings beside the parsley in the Styrofoam planter that so offends the High Cockalorum. Predictably, she came along last year just as I was patting down the soil around the transplants' roots. She snorted audibly. *"Hmpf."* Politely, I asked her if she'd like some basil—there's always enough to spare. "Heavens no. I only plant the purple kind." And off she went. I could only sigh, keep on setting the basil in its summer bed, and wish fervently that she be attacked by pimples and pumples.

I'm certain that the HC does not know the whole basil story: fit for a king, fit also for a commoner. Its binomial is formed of two latinized Greek words, *Ocimum basilicum,* which means "king's basil." And it was anciently introduced into the Mediterranean from its native haunts in India and Iran. Pliny mentions it, recommending that it be planted on April 21 at the Feast of Pales, the female tutelary spirit whose watch it was to preside over cattle and pastures. He says that basil starts to yellow when Sirius, the dog star, rises in the month of August and brings on wilting heat. According to him, there's another circumstance that makes all plants turn yellow: the approach of a *mulier mentrualis,* a menstruating woman. I want to shout at him across the millennia that this business about female blood and bollixed plants is just not true. But Pliny was ever credulous, ever quick to report the most outlandish rumors. The dear man assures us that there is a sea turtle in the Indian Ocean with a shell big enough for people to use as a boat or a house; he believes, as well, in Nereids with hairy bodies like seals and Tritons that blow mournful tunes on trumpet shells held in their horse forelegs. In Pliny's time basil was not a culinary herb but one employed in the service of medicine. Even into the early seventeenth century of John Gerard basil was an item in the pharmacopoeia rather than the kitchen spice rack. Gerard quotes Dioscorides, another Greek physician, contemporary to Pliny and author of *De Materia Medica,* the earliest surviving text on pharmaceuticals and their uses: "Dioscorides saith that if Basill be much eaten, it dulleth the sight, it mollifieth the belly, breedeth winde, provoketh urine, drieth up milk, and is of hard digestion." Gerard himself says nothing of basil's flavor; rather he recommends mixing the plant's juice with wine to cure a headache and using the juice straight to clean away dimness of the eyes. The seeds, too, may effect cures: "The seed drunke is a remedie for melancholicke people, for those that are short winded, and them that can hardly make water." And if you need to sneeze, well, there's nothing better than sniffing the seeds up your nose. To give him credit, Gerard does praise the smell of basil, which is "good for the heart and for the head." Oh, yes! One of the delights of growing basil is producing leaves to dry. Forget air fresheners: Five tiers of leaves in the dehydrator fill our trailer with their brisk green scent.

Basil has also been put to peculiar uses—or so says the poet John Keats, setting to verse a gruesome tale from Boccaccio. The poem is "Isabella; or, The Pot of Basil," and it recounts a story of murder and transformation. Isabella's true love, Lorenzo, was killed and buried in a dim forest by her brothers, proud Florentine merchants who had wished to marry her off to a rich man. Once home again, they lied and told Isabella that Lorenzo had shipped out to attend to their affairs in a foreign land. But he did not return, and still he did not return. Yet he appeared to her in a vision, dirt encrusted and moaning "a ghostly under-song."

And he asked her to find his grave and there shed one tear to comfort him. So Isabella, in the company of an aged nurse, hied herself to the forest, where they uncovered the corpse, cut off his head, and took it home. After Isabella had combed its hair and kissed it, the head was placed in a pot of basil. And the basil thrived:

> And so she ever fed it with thin tears,
>> Whence thick, and green, and beautiful it grew,
> So that it smelt more balmy than its peers
>> Of Basil-tufts in Florence; for it drew
> Nurture besides, and life, from human fears,
>> From the fast moldering head there shut from view:
> So that the jewel, safely casketed,
>> Came forth and in perfumed leafits spread.

The evil brothers steal the pot, of course; wan, lovelorn Isabella languishes and dies. The poem ends.

But basil itself does not end, neither in idea or reality. The poem, moreover, contravenes reality in one dire respect: Those tears would not have pleased the herb, for it does not like dampness. It is an aromatic annual amorous of the sun. And I am amorous of basil.

Accidents may bring blessings. My herb garden at Great Neck Point is one of those. Dispersed among planters and pots, and a patch of earth here, another there, it brings me bees and butterflies, fragrances and flavors to keep or give away at Christmastime. It makes gladness spring sweet and green in my heart.

HIGH SUMMER: ANTAIOS'S CHILDREN

WEEDS AREN'T POLITE. Never were and never will be. Once upon a time, the Old English word *weod,* from which we get *weed,* meant "any herb or small plant," but the current definition refers to a plant that is not wanted but insists on having its own way. It finds its strength in touching earth. Come drought or downpour, it thrusts its roots down firmly, grows with indecent speed, elbows more retiring greenery aside, and sets prodigious amounts of seeds.

Weeds have been with us ever since we clambered out of our hunting-gathering niche and settled down to raise crops in permanent gardens. In Book I of his *Georgics* the Roman poet Virgil writes that from the misty, mythic time when Ceres, the corn goddess, taught men how to till the soil with an iron plow, wild fruits became scarce in the sacred groves, and the gods no longer granted food just for the picking.

> Soon, the labor of growing corn increased, foul molds
> infected the stalks, and the thistle sent shock troops
> into the fields: crops fail, a rough forest pushes up—
> burs and star-thistles, unproductive rye grass
> and sterile wild oats lord it over the bright furrows.

The only recourse is to attack the weeds with an unremitting hoe. Else the farmer will find that the only food available is acorns shaken down from oak trees.

Weeds! Because the garden in New Field is fairly well tilled, at least between the rows (the Chief, whose back was giving him bother, hired a handyman), I can keep up with the would-be squatters, like Virginia creeper and rabbit tobacco and several kinds of morning-glory, but oh, the plot in Garden Field is ever rich in greedy weeds that do, if given a smidgen of a chance, wage undeclared war against the vegetables, casting tall shade over them and starving them out. They are Antaios's children, gaining strength from touching their mother earth—and I am Herakles, determined to root them out. Early on I use a hoe. Later, when the weeds have started gaining ground, I use hands and dandelion digger to lift them into the air. I plop them into a five-gallon bucket and, when the bucket's full, dump them into the Will-Be. (That's our name for the tall black compost bin in Garden Field; the Has-Bin for recyclables sits on the front deck.) Weeds are good for something after all: enriching soil—if, that is, they haven't begun to set seeds.

Weeding is a time for remembering gardens: the first Justamere garden to which I proudly drove so that dozens of ears of corn could be brought to the Big House and, a decade later, a second Justamere garden that I planted as a grown woman. My husband and I, with newborn first child, moved from the city to the farm so that we could act as its caretakers. He cut the acres of lawn and maintained the dirt roads; I dealt with the tenants. The farmer, no longer farming, still lived with his family in their cottage, but three of the other houses were rented, sometimes happily, sometimes not. We ourselves lived in the Dutch Colonial water tower. No longer did its tank hold water, and my father's still, installed on the ground level, had been packed up and put away. A wing had been added, converting the tower into a house. Our small daughter slept in the tower as if she were a fairy-tale princess. And I began to garden. The horse barn yielded an old high-wheel cultivator with long wooden handles and earth-turning tines set behind a large wheel. It was easy to push through the soil. Behold—a small vegetable plot beside a row of apple trees. One of the tenants gave me a tip: Plant tomato seeds when the apple blossoms pop, for then the soil of north-central Ohio is warm enough. For several years, the tomatoes, red rosy tomatoes, were spectacular and succulent. Then, with a second child, the enchanted tower house became too small, and we moved back to the city.

The next garden arose in Connecticut, six miles inland from Long Island Sound. I should say gardens, for we grew not only vegetables—including those for which second daughter won prizes—but also flowers. And there, in pursuit of flowers, I learned a precept about weeding. Our large lot held lawn, a sizable blackberry thicket, a woods with spindly third-growth trees, and hundreds of feet of New England stone walls. After contemplating the stones for several years, after removing the poison ivy that festooned them, I thought they needed color. So began the big swap. I ran an ad in the local paper offering to trade my excess perennials—pinks, dwarf iris, hens-and-chicks—for orange daylilies. Their flame would illuminate those mousy gray walls. The telephone rang steadily for four weeks, long after the ad itself had disappeared. Not only did the plain roadside daylilies come our way but also oranges with double petals and a glowing collection of tetraploid hybrids—pink, peach, yellow, maroon with gold stripes. Small daylilies and large, they bloomed along those drab walls from April into September. Of course, I visited the gardens of the traders. It was one of them, a spry retiree, who gave me instruction in weeding. Though he grew other things, he specialized in breeding azaleas, and when I came to call his hillside plot was softly ablaze with color. He gave me a tour to introduce me to his favorites. Along the way he took hold of various bits of greenery and uprooted them. "Weeds," he said, "but I never pull 'em up till they're tall enough so I don't have to bend over to get 'em." Ah, wait until the weeds are waist high! To this day, I apply his good, back-saving advice to certain of Antaios's children. Ragweed is an ideal candidate: When it has grown within easy reach, the stem is tough enough so that pulling does not break it; the plant comes up roots and all.

Weeding is also a time for rumination, for chewing over puzzles until they're full of holes and light shines through. The hands work on automatic; the brain goes into dolphin mode, rolling along in slow motion just under the surface of thought. Often, problems solve themselves. I understand the mechanism here: Gaining distance from a conundrum can lead to a clearer view of the path toward a solution. The things that I contemplate range from the elementary to those that affect the course of our lives. How do I make that complicated knitting stitch? How shall I ease from one topic to the next in the piece I'm currently writing? Shall we rebuild the pier swept away four years ago by a vicious winter nor'easter? Or, certain of nor'easters to come, leave well enough alone and not risk another loss? And what can the Chief and I reasonably do to help clean up an increasingly polluted river or to preserve the area's much-diminished habitat for nesting birds? We hope, both of us, to have our ashes cast into the river. Would that be an act of heedless pollution? Might we not be better off strewn over the garden, where our slight remains could marry the soil without injury to anything else, be it plant, turtle, or garden spider? With the dandelion digger, I uproot weeds, cast them into a bucket, and consider my own full-ripened life.

And weeding, as it happens, is a time for visiting. The owner of Cockadoodle-Stew comes to rake up the haylike clippings of dried grass in New Field for use as mulch in her garden. Other neighbors stroll by on their daily constitutionals. One is Dorothy, whose raised-bed garden features vegetables and more, including the heartiest, most carefully nurtured milkweed plants that I've ever seen. Another is Becky's father, Mo, possessor of a truly green thumb; he has not only gardened on a scale grand enough to feed a family of five but also grown things like basil and elephant garlic in a now-beached skiff he once used in commercial fishing. In one of my first encounters with him, he remarked, most memorably, "Planting a seed, you can't deny the hope that goes with it." Becky herself may stop by on a weekend.

The High Cockalorum comes along one morning as I'm yanking a bunch of Mexican clover out of the double row of wax beans. "How you doin'?" I ask. She stands there watching me for a good minute before she replies. Then it's not "I'm fine," but rather "Lots of weeds." I barely begin to identify the clump in hand as Mexican clover before she interrupts. "I keep my garden clean." And away she goes.

My bile rises. Yank! Weeding helps divert feelings of aggression.

But Lord knows, I'm not perfect. I'm lazy, and there's no excusing it on the grounds that I've earned my leisure after living nearly seven decades and rearing four children. I procrastinate (don't all writers procrastinate?), putting off till tomorrow and the day after

that various pesky things—cleaning the bathtub, folding the laun-
dry—that could very well be done in ten minutes. And I should
know better, for the ten minutes gets shoved into the future, where
it looms like a boulder blocking the way between me and things that
take much more time but always bring delight—picking basil and
setting it out to dry, sitting on the front deck watching dolphins as
I stem the beans, reading cookbooks and stirring up something new
to feed the Chief at supper. But sometimes I ignore him because
I'm lost in the fifth century B.C., or the gardens at Monticello, or
(worst-case scenario) a computer game. I'm also given to an occasional fib (note how that's qualified by *occasional*). It's not outright
mendacity, though, but rather saying, "Oh, sure," when I definitely
think the opposite and telling someone that I don't really see the
weeds in her garden or mine. And all my writing is subjective,
reflecting not eternal truth but truth as I see it. Instead of verity, I
specialize in verisimilitude and have been known to rearrange events
to make an account seem more persuasive. But I'm not—please
God, I never shall be—a high cockalorum.

Yank! And I find myself contemplating the weed in my hand. A
thousand Mexican clover plants infest the rows of beans. Yet they're
not unattractive. Vividly green leaves like pair after pair of lightly
furry little wings sprout densely from fat stems that have a propen-
sity to bend and trail. Come bloom time in August the flowers will
look like clusters of small, six-pointed white stars, and come August
I'll happily let it bloom, for the beans are done by then. But possessed by an active itch to know more about what I'm dealing with,
I look up Mexican clover's particulars when I'm back inside. The
same itch makes me want to know the names of birds, trees, fish,
and rocks, so that they cease to be strangers and can be regarded as

acquaintances, if not as friends. The plant turns out to be not a real clover but rather a member of the madder family, which includes wildflowers like bluets and dye plants like bedstraw. Science, in the person of Linnaeus himself, has dubbed it *Richardia scabra,* "Richard's rough plant." Just who, pray tell, was Richard? None of my books names such a person; so, going farther afield, I send the question to the botanical library at the University of North Carolina. Ah, he was one Richard Richardson (1663–1741), a physician. According to one description, "During most of his life he was only nominally attached to the practice of medicine, but he was able to indulge his botanical tastes, in the pursuit of which he traveled over most of England, Wales, and Scotland." His personal garden was said to be "probably the finest private garden in England." Taxonomical custom often latinizes the names of notable amateurs and professionals and thus honors their achievements in various fields by including the names in binomials. But why attach his name—or the name of any human being—to something as obnoxious as Mexican clover? I learn that the plant is not universally regarded as a weed; happiest in dry, sandy soils, it's sown as a forage crop. Well, that helps explain its presence in the sandy loam of Garden Field. As for the name, it is obliged to have one in the not unreasonable view of science. Furthermore, an honor is an honor, no matter to what plant or animal it appends.

Yank!

But as the season wears on, Antaios's children begin to take command. The 10–10–10 fertilizer that the Chief applied to squashes, tomatoes, and beans is sucked up just as eagerly by weeds. By mid-July some of the more obstreperous begin to tower over the vegetables: time to grub out the ragweed, which especially likes the section of the

garden where the butternut vines sprawl from the little hills in which
the seeds were planted back in May when the soil had warmed. The
advice gained in Connecticut long ago comes in handy: It's easiest to
weed when you don't have to bend over. I wait for a sunny morning
after a night of sozzling rain, and off to the squash patch I go. Each
three-foot-tall ragweed is a forest of delicately incised leaves. But I
grasp the stout stems firmly and tug them loose. They do not go into
the Will-Be; they'd clog it. So I toss them into the field at the side of
the garden and later complete the execution by running over them
with the lawn tractor, mower at full throttle. They're villains anyhow;
it's the yellow pollen of their flowers that brings on the miseries of hay
fever.

Yet the plant intrigues me. And its scientific name has a romantic
ring: *Ambrosia artemisiifolia,* "wormwood-leaved food of the gods."
Wormwood is a member of the genus *Artemisia,* which derives its
name from Artemis, goddess of the moon, the hunt, and the keeping
of chastity. Ragweed's lacy leaves do resemble those of wormwood,
but I cannot guess the reason that it and some other weedy herbs,
none of them palatable, were given a generic name that points to
ambrosia, one of the divine comestibles—the other was nectar—
atop Mount Olympus. But for all the sneezes and swollen sinuses
ragweed causes, it is not entirely baneful, at least not in the realm
of folk medicine. A bunch of leaves put in your pocket is said to
alleviate the agonies of being galded—of being chafed, that is. Once
upon a time not long ago, the Chief stayed up all night to clean a
great run of bluefish that had hurled themselves into a neighbor's
gill net; when dawn came, his inner thighs were chafed raw from
moving about for hour after hour in a wet jumpsuit. When another
neighbor said the word *galded* and suggested the ragweed treatment,

he snorted. "Galded? More like gelded." But he went out, dutifully gathered some ragweed, and stuffed it in the pockets of his jeans. He'll swear to this day that it works.

When August rolls in, hot and steamy, only tomatoes, butternut vines, and eggplants are still producing. The peppers will bear fruit again come cooler weather, but now they droop. So do I. Then Antaios's children begin most forcefully to assert themselves. And I find myself wondering about them. Collected, they are layered in paper toweling and pressed between the pages of Gerard's *Herball,* which has the heft of an unabridged dictionary. When they're dry enough, I bag them, put them in an envelope, and send them off to the county's cooperative extension agent or the botanist at the North Carolina Maritime Museum. They are expert at identifying weeds: the native sicklepod, the leafflower that came this way from its original home in tropical east Asia, and a host of others, both indigenous and alien. I think again about how peaceably the out-landers mix with plants that have been here since the beginning of weedtime in the New World. Rascally though they be, weeds quietly mind their own business. Competition exists, no doubt about that, and it's lively, but it usually does not reach a state of internecine war-fare. Among the plants, I see altogether better behavior than that among my own kind. No Bosnias or Kosovos for them; no Rwandas.

With each new identification, I keep watch on the weeds as they grow and bloom and form their fruits. How easy it is to overlook the obvious! It took me fifteen years to notice sicklepod, which starts its growing modestly—a little plant with rounded leaflets one on top of another like an opened fan. Then it shoots up and out, becoming a tender bush four or more feet in height. Its blossoms are small and yellow, each one hiding alone in the juncture of leaf with stem. The fruit is most curious—a slender, lightly curved pod no bigger around than a number five knitting needle and a good five or six inches long. The first time that I became aware of the plant, I knew that it was a member of the bean family, because of the pealike leaves. But other than that, I knew nothing. A few plucked leaves were quickly inserted into the middle of *The Herball.* The extension agent pronounced it to be *Cassia obtusifolia,* which means "blunt-leaved senna." Some of its African and Near Eastern kin are used medicinally, particularly for their purgative action. I doubt, however, that the senna in our garden has any human uses—except to give me something new to contemplate.

Leafflower, a member of the spurge family, took up residence in the United States in the early 1940s. Its common name is a direct translation of its Greek generic name, *Phyllanthus;* its species is *urinaria,* about which more shall be said in a moment. The fruits of this weed are even more peculiar than those of sicklepod. Tiny flowers are attached singly to the stem immediately below the leaves, and seed capsules nearly the size of peppercorns form directly on the stem as if the stem had been strung with many hard little beads. *Urinaria* refers to a few of the plant's medicinal properties, its use as a diuretic and as a remedy for infections of the urinary tract. It's also reputed to be the base of effective treatments for a slew of ailments, from jaundice, diabetes, and gonorrhea to asthma and baldness. In India the root has been given to sleepless children to send them into their dreams, and there traditional fishermen prepare a fish poison from the whole plant. In our garden, though, it grows only as a curiosity.

Weeds—many communities have laws against weeds. If we lived somewhere other than Great Neck Point, where chickens roam through neighboring yards and brush piles rise like green hillocks in the middle of unkempt fields, the weed police might well consider us lawbreakers. The rationale behind setting up laws against weeds is that the very existence of weeds growing abundantly in yards or vacant lots leads ipso facto to a slumgullion of undesirable conditions: The lot might catch on fire, shelter rats, provide breeding grounds for mosquitoes, and send off great clouds of noxious pollens on the wind to smother the allergic. Even worse, perhaps, is that some legislators have made comparisons between manicured lawns and those that look overgrown and find the latter sadly lacking in beauty and propriety. My Illinois daughter-in-law has faced the weed police several times on the last count—and faced them down, because she grows protected prairie plants in her postage-stamp front yard. As for the other complaints, grass and weed fires are too short lived to burn down houses. Then, rats don't live amid weeds; it's barns and garbage dumps that provide them with the steady food supply they need. Nor do mosquitoes breed anywhere but in pools of standing water; depending on the species, a minimum of ten days is required to complete the life cycle. And pollen—morning-glories, jimson, and Mexican clover never made anyone sneeze, never clogged sinuses and brought on pounding headaches. Only ragweed is the villain here. Or rather, we are the villains, for ragweed likes disturbed places. A garden, tilled and cultivated every year, offers it an ideal place to hang out.

After August, Antaios's children gleefully take over our garden plots. The ragweed (I never manage to get it all) grows eight feet tall, a testimonial to the power of 10–10–10 fertilizer. Mexican clover makes a lush green carpet where the bean rows used to be. Sicklepod attains the height of a high-bush blueberry. Next thing I know, I'm taking inventory of our weeds.

The outlanders, the exotics that have sneaked in from other places, other times, are not so numerous as the natives. But they're plentiful enough. Most of them came in from the Tropics of the New World, while a few arrived on these shores from Eurasia or Asia proper. And here are the companions of Mexican clover and leaf-flower, the aliens already mentioned:

- amaranth, also called redroot pigweed, *Amaranthus retroflexus,* annual, native to tropical America
- Bermuda grass, *Cynodon dactylon,* perennial, native to the Mediterranean
- bindweed, field, *Convolvulus arvensis,* perennial, native to Europe
- carpetweed, also called Indian-chickweed, *Mollugo verticillata,* annual, native to tropical America
- chickweed, common, *Stellaria media,* annual, probably native to Europe
- chickweed, mouse-ear, *Cerastium glomeratum,* winter annual, native to Europe
- crabgrass, *Digitaria* spp., annual, native to Europe
- cypress vine, *Ipomoea quamoclit,* annual, native to tropical America
- dandelion, *Taraxacum officinale,* perennial, native to Eurasia
- dayflower, Asiatic, *Commelina communis,* annual, native to eastern Asia
- dock, curly, *Rumex crispus,* perennial, native to Eurasia
- Indian strawberry, *Duchesnea indica,* perennial, native to Asia
- jimsonweed, also called thorn apple, *Datura stramonium,* annual of mysterious origins, perhaps Peru or farther afield in the Old World's Tropics

- lamb's-quarters, also called pigweed or goosefoot, *Chenopodium album,* annual, native to Eurasia
- low hop clover, *Trifolium campestre,* annual or biennial, native to Eurasia and northern Africa
- onion, wild, also called wild garlic or field garlic, *Allium vineale,* perennial, native to Europe
- pennywort, Asiatic, *Centella asiatica,* perennial, native to Asia
- plantain, common, *Plantago major,* perennial, sometimes annual, native to Eurasia, although botanists speculate that it may also be native to North America
- quack grass, *Agropyron repens,* perennial, native to Europe
- star-of-Bethlehem, *Ornithogalum umbellatum,* perennial, native to Europe
- thistle, sow, *Sonchus* spp., annual, native to Europe
- trefoil, bird's-foot, also called cat-clover, *Lotus corniculatus,* annual, native to Europe
- vetch, narrow-leaved, *Vicia angustifolia,* annual, native to Europe
- wart-cress, also called carpet-cress, *Coronopus didyma,* annual, native to South America

Although many of these weeds were stowaways, others came here honorably. Dandelion, chickweed, and jimsonweed were part of the pharmacopoeia of the English settlers. John Gerard mentions all three in his *Herball.* Low hop clover and narrow-leaved vetch were introduced in colonial times as forage crops. As for lamb's-quarters, I suspect that it was one of the stowaways. I know for a fact that its leaves are delicious. Pick the young shoots, strip the leaves from the stems, cook them as you would spinach—no water to speak of, and add lots of butter: The result tastes like fresh spinach but has none of the grit that always comes with homegrown spinach—store-bought spinach, too, for that matter. The plant also indicates the condition of the soil: A nitrogen deficiency gives lamb's-quarters' leaves a reddish sheen.

One of the imports that flourishes in our garden—and in gardens, fields, and waste places throughout the United States—is downright poisonous: jimsonweed, which belongs—with tomatoes, potatoes, and eggplant—to the nightshade family. Because its round seedpods are covered with prickles, it's earned the name *thorn apple.* John Gerard calls it thorne-apple and mentions a specimen brought to him from Constantinople. And just how did an alien plant receive a common name that refers to a place in Virginia? The reason for its assignment to Jamestown is that an early Virginian, Robert Beverly, wrote in his *History and Present State of Virginia* about a misadventure suffered at that settlement in 1676 by some soldiers, who were simply looking for greens to put in their bellies. The plant, which he called James-Town-Weed,

> was gather'd very young for boil'd Salad, by some of the
> Soldiers sent thither . . . and some of them eat plentifully
> of it, the Effect of which was a very pleasant Comedy;
> for they turn'd Fools upon it for several days: One
> would blow up a Feather in the Air; another woul'd dart
> Straws at it with much Fury; and another stark naked
> was sitting in a Corner, like a Monkey, grinning and
> making Mows at them; a Fourth would fondly kiss, and
> paw his Companions, and snear in their Faces. . . . In
> this frantick Condition they were confined, lest they
> should in their Folly destroy themselves. . . . A thousand

such simple Tricks they play'd, and after Eleven Days, return'd to themselves again, not remembering anything that had pass'd.

The soldiers had tripped out on the plant's hallucinogenic alkaloids. And to this day, jimsonweed is so used by people looking for a high. In the early '80s, when I volunteered as leader of a creative writing workshop in a maximum-security prison for men, some of my students told horrific tales about prisoners, particularly those working on the highways, who picked the weed and put it in their pockets to take back to their quarters for happy hour. More often than not the effect was that of a heavy binge or, worse, near-to-death delirium. They were lucky: Jimsonweed can kill.

The inventory rolls on, this time with the North American weeds that flourish with great élan in most of the gardens at the Point. It's a motley bunch of opportunists, some of which are rank and rowdy, while one is downright delicious and a few others are—yes, they are—damned beautiful. Ragweed and sicklepod have been mentioned already; here, except for a clutch of hard-to-identify grasses, are their lusty companions:

- ➤ beggar-ticks, *Bidens frondosa,* annual
- ➤ betony, Florida, *Stachys floridana,* perennial
- ➤ bitter cress, *Cardamine hirsuta,* winter annual
- ➤ blackberry, also called bramble, *Rubus* spp., perennial
- ➤ blue-eyed grass, *Sisyrinchum angustifolium,* perennial
- ➤ corn-salad, *Valerianella radiata,* annual
- ➤ cinquefoil, common, *Potentilla simplex,* perennial
- ➤ cranesbill, Carolina, *Geranium carolinianum,* annual

- ➤ dog fennel, or summer cedar, *Eupatorium capillifolium,* annual
- ➤ evening primrose, common, *Oenothera biennis,* biennial
- ➤ evening primrose, cutleaf, *Oenothera laciniata,* biennial
- ➤ fleabane, common, or daisy fleabane, *Erigeron philadelphicus,* biennial
- ➤ greenbrier, also called catbrier, *Smilax bona-nox,* perennial
- ➤ ground-cherry, *Physalis* spp., perennial
- ➤ henbit, *Lamium amplexicaule,* biennial
- ➤ lespedeza, *Lespedeza* spp., perennial
- ➤ lettuce, wild, *Lactuca serriola,* annual
- ➤ mist flower, *Eupatorium coelestinum,* perennial
- ➤ morning-glory, ivy-leaved, *Ipomoea hederacea,* annual
- ➤ nightshade, also called horse nettle, *Solanum carolinense,* annual
- ➤ poison ivy, *Rhus radicans,* woody perennial
- ➤ pokeweed, *Phytolacca americana,* perennial
- ➤ potato vine, wild, *Ipomoea pandurata,* annual
- ➤ rabbit tobacco, *Pseudognaphalium obtusifolium,* annual
- ➤ ragwort, golden, or golden groundsel, *Senecio aureus,* perennial
- ➤ sage, lyre-leaved, *Salvia lyrata,* perennial
- ➤ St.-Andrew's-cross, *Ascyrum hypericoides* (some botanists deem it *Hypericum hypericoides,* in the same genus as St.-John's-wort), annual
- ➤ sedge, umbrella, *Cyperus strigosus,* perennial
- ➤ sheep sorrel, *Rumex acetosella,* perennial
- ➤ smartweed, *Polygonum pensylvanicum,* annual
- ➤ sorrel, *Rumex hastatulus,* annual
- ➤ spurge, spotted, *Chamaecyce maculata,* annual
- ➤ star grass, yellow, *Hypoxis hirsuta,* perennial
- ➤ thistle, yellow, *Cirsium horridulum,* biennial

- ➤ toadflax, blue, also known as old-field toadflax, *Linaria canadensis,* biennial or winter annual
- ➤ trumpet creeper, *Campsis radicans,* woody perennial
- ➤ Venus's-looking-glass, *Specularia perfoliata,* annual
- ➤ Virginia creeper, *Parthenocissus quinquefolia,* perennial
- ➤ wood sorrel, yellow, *Oxalis stricta,* perennial

No one honors poison ivy. You must be careful, too, with wild potato vine and ivy-leaved morning-glory; they're not so civilized as their close cousin, *I. batatas,* the sweet potato, nor are they in the slightest edible. Instead they wind around tomato cages, march up pole bean supports, and smother the works. Spotted spurge is rather belligerent, too, spreading rapidly into a thick, hard-to-root-out mat. Then, of the prickly plants, I could do without all but one. If it were possible, I'd banish forever the yellow thistle—it's a bully— and banish the beggar-ticks that stick tight in my socks and the legs of my pants and must be extracted slowly afterward, and banish also from our garden's commonwealth the nightshade that, like its close cousin jimsonweed, specializes in thin, sharp needles but bears them on its stems rather than on its fruits. If you aren't wearing gloves, beware when you try to pull it up; the barehanded secret, though, is to grasp the plant where it has no thorns, at the point where the stem emerges from the earth. But thorny though it is, the blackberry is invited to stay, if not in the garden proper, at least on its periphery. The reasons are simple: cobbler, pie, jam.

Many of the others also have virtues. For each plant described in *The Herball,* Gerard supplies a list of "Vertues." I take the word in his sense to mean "the possession of special efficacy in some respect." Pokeweed's squishy purple berries are relished by the birds; so are the smaller, harder fruits of Virginia creeper, on which I've seen flickers hanging upside down to feed. Pokeweed, incidentally, has made a reverse migration, west to east, across the Atlantic, but I do not know if it figures on European lists of pest plants. Hummingbirds visit the trumpetlike orange flowers of the trumpet creeper. Cottontail rabbits feast on wild lettuce, both that in the garden and that in our somewhat shaggy back lawn; we have photographs of one aged bunny, blind in one eye, that lay down to do her chomping. As for rabbit tobacco, cottontails eat it, but children (like, once upon a time, the Chief) use it otherwise. Lured by the glamour of smoking but too young to buy cigarettes, they roll the dried leaves in newspaper and light up. Corn-salad is a people crop. *Corn* is the English term for "wheat," and the plant's name refers to greens gathered in wheat fields for human consumption. It was anciently cultivated; archaeologists have found seeds of at least two species in Swiss lake dwellings. The European settlers, noting a kind of corn-salad in the New World, knew right away what to call it and brought it into their kitchen gardens. I happily nibble on the plant in Garden Field when it pops up in April. Wood sorrel is people food, too, at least where I'm concerned; its fresh-picked leaves add a delightful note of sourness to a tossed salad. Also good to eat are the berries contained in the lanterns—the husks, that is—of ground-cherries, which may be turned into excellent jellies and jams; they are, after all, close relatives of the tomato. And the evening primrose, which easily tolerates poor soil, may be considered a root vegetable, and plant breeders have even developed cultivars for vegetable gardens; I'm not sure that I'm adventurous enough to try eating it, for the root's flavor is said to be unpleasantly peppery. Umbrella sedge, which belongs to the same genus as papyrus, has edible relatives; in Africa a variety of the hearty weed that infests our Great Neck gardens is actually cultivated for its nutritious tuber. It looks like grass but is easily identified as a sedge by its triangular stem (a helpful mnemonic advises that "sedges have edges"). Mouse-ear chickweed, as softly fuzzy as a plush toy, soothes my fingers. And St.-Andrew's-cross, its four-petaled yellow flowers resting lightly, gaily at the tips of long, leafy stems, is said to have the stress-relieving properties of St.-John's-wort.

Virtues, yes. And none are more virtuous, I think, than those that may be appreciated as wildflowers. Oh, they run rampant through our gardens, they rage amid the vegetables, but nonetheless they do it so quietly and with such elegance that I am softly stunned with admiration. There's evening primrose with its short-lived but showy blossoms the color of butter, and common fleabane, a member of the daisy family, whirling its fine lavender petals around a golden eye. In May blue toadflax conspires with sorrel to cover the weedy green of fallow fields with a wash of lavender and rose. In the same month Venus must surely pause here to admire herself in the mirrors of blue-violet flowers that nestle cozily in the leaf axils on a foot-high stem. Then, unlike its plush and far gaudier geranium cousins that are sold in garden marts, Carolina cranesbill with its deeply incised leaves and small pale purple blossoms exhibits a graceful modesty. And lyre-leaved sage, in the same genus as the sage I cook with, lifts high its crown of pale pink flowers from a dark green basal rosette; it does not invade the garden proper but crowds close and abundant along the edges.

There's one weed I not only admire but also encourage: cypress vine, one of the immigrants from tropical America. The plant is glorious—slender, pliant stems covered with fine, feathery leaves resembling those of bald cypress, and scarlet flowers like pinwheels no bigger around than a dime. We met it in deep summer during the first year that we grew vegetables in Garden Field. It had climbed a tomato cage and alerted us to its presence by bursting into full red bloom. We were astonished. Becky's father, Mo, was able to tell us that it was a morning-glory, but he couldn't put a name to it. I photographed it and sent the snapshots to the botanist at the North Carolina Maritime Museum, twenty-five miles down the road. Ah, *Ipomoea quamoclit!* The designation for the genus translates as "worm-like," for the winding habit of its tendrils; the one for the species is that used as a common name in Mexico and comes, I'm sure, from an indigenous language. Since the cypress vine first offered its feathery leaves to the sun and lit its soft red fire in our garden, I've learned to spot the plants when they're tiny. An area is set aside, one or two tomato cages are placed over the seedlings, and they climb, then blaze gently and continually from midsummer till the first hard chills of autumn. Their company is bright and splendid. As it happens, other people, seeing them amid the tomatoes, also desire their company. There are enough seeds to go around, to share with others and to settle in our garden for growing next year and the year after. So we give little bags of cypress-vine-to-be to all who wish to introduce the feathery leaves and brilliant little flowers into their own gardens.

Nor are these all of the weeds that we support. I'm sure that hosts of others, some retiring and some unpleasantly surly, will reveal themselves in years to come. And the questions arise, each one as stubborn as a weed: What good are these intruders, these invaders that rush in like conquerors to possess turned earth? What is their purpose in this world? And how do I, with my guerrilla warfare, fit into the greater scheme of things? Like it or not, I am obliged to share my territory with a host of other lives.

The best answer comes, I think, from Aldo Leopold, the forester and ecologist who proposed a land ethic back in the 1940s. He writes: "All ethics so far evolved rest upon a single premise: that the individual is a member of a community of interdependent parts. His instincts prompt him to compete for his place in that community, but his ethics prompt him also to co-operate (perhaps in order that there may be a place to compete for). The land ethic simply enlarges the boundaries of the community to include soils, waters, plants, and animals, or collectively, the land." Community, then, is more than a social contract among people. It includes the whole of creation, the things that we don't like as well as those that we do. Deerflies keep company with monarch butterflies and luna moths, cowbirds and starlings with warblers and woodpeckers, stingrays with flounder and blue crabs, ragweed, nightshade, and Mexican clover with beans and squash. And we are part of those communities, fellow travelers with fish and birds, bugs and weeds—indeed, with the entire sprawling, pushing, tumultuous entanglements of life. The competition is often intense. Here, in the garden, I am forced to ponder the not-so-simple fact that we're all here on the same stage—planet earth—where we all spend our lives in the instinctive quest for food and reproductive success. Humankind is forever claiming rights on its own behalf and those of the animals, like whales and chimps, that we find desirable. But is there anyone who advocates rights for laboratory rats, fruit flies, or weeds? I think not. It's clear that assessing the goodness, mediocrity, or outright undesirability of any living thing is a matter of perception. The trumpet creeper illustrates the case. This plant that willy-nilly overruns the South, climbing trees and covering fences with a boldness just a little less extreme than that of kudzu, was bought intentionally and set in the earth to climb a trellis by the porte cochère at Justamere Farm. I remember the glow of its tubular flowers as they peeped through the second-floor windows.

The weeds take over the garden almost totally by the beginning of September. I continue to clear them away from the vegetables, the eggplants and bell peppers, that still produce. But the rest of the garden is theirs. Now *I* become the weed, intruding on their domain. (It may be that my kind is the world's most aggressive weed. And I know for certain that the High Cockalorum intrudes like a weed in the garden of my sensibilities.) Come October, though, cypress vine, Mexican clover, jimson, spurge, and all the others will be gone, for the Chief will have given the sandy loam a deep tilling. Next year, of course, the weeds will rise again en masse, their numbers undiminished. Like fish, like insects, their reproductive strategy relies on the production of uncountable small packets of genes. To assure the survival of a future generation, their seeds number easily in the millions. For all those that fail, that are eaten or drowned or gone moldy, others—not so many but enough—will sprout and root and reach for heaven. As long as we have a garden or, more likely, as long as we have the energy to plant a garden, I shall not let the weeds elbow out the food plants till our crop is in. After that, I bow to their vigor and endurance.

Goodness knows, the garden—the world—has room enough for all of us.

QUEEN MAB'S WAGGON

LEAVES RUSTLE, LIGHT GLINTS; out of the corner of my eye I am aware of almost constant movement. We share our garden—vegetables, herbs, flowers, and weeds—not just with rabbits, turtles, snakes, and snails but also with a leap of grasshoppers, a glitter of dragonflies, a scamper of centipedes, and more, myriads more. They may be shy or bold, drab and unobtrusive or patterned with colorful see-me designs. Today I find, as I'd hoped, that a favorite has moved in. She seems the garden's chatelaine, keeper of its small but mighty secrets.

It must have been last evening that she suspended her orb web between the leaves of a tall, caged tomato vine. This morning she rests at web's center in her full yellow-and-black splendor. And oh, what an intricate web she spins! The radii, some a good ten inches long, are connected by a fine, closely spun spiral of sticky silk. In the center another kind of silk decorates the web—a slim vertical band of cottony white zigzags. Amid this intricate spinning, she waits. Patience, patience: The next meal—a fly, a grasshopper?—will bump into the net and stick fast to its gluey strands.

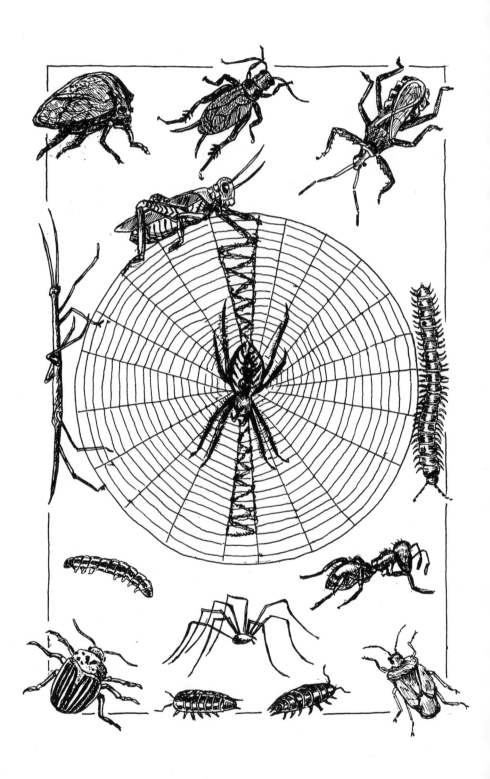

She's a garden spider, the familiar black-and-yellow argiope. Science calls her kind *Argiope aurantia,* the "golden bright-face." The genus name summons Argiope of Greek myth, who mothered Cadmus, founder of Thebes, and also Europa, victim of Zeus's divine and restless lust; the name of a continent now honors her. The spider's long, egg-shaped body gleams against the backdrop of green leaves. Her slender reddish legs wear bands of black. With half a bucket of tomatoes still to be picked, I pause to watch her and to wonder at her web. The characteristic zigzag arrangement is called a stabilimentum, which means "stabilizer, stay, support." But its true purpose baffles scientists. It may indeed serve to hold things together, or it may be camouflage, intended to fool predators. The latter seems unlikely, though, for the spider often positions herself head-down at web center amid the zigzags as if she were using them to draw attention to her artful silken construct and, indeed, to herself. Experiments conducted in the United States indicate that stabilimenta may well be warning signs for birds: A web in place indicates a no-fly zone. It takes considerable protein for her—for any spider —to spin a web, and its destruction by bird, or human being, means that the silk is lost forever, a loss that's physically costly to the spinner, which would otherwise recycle the protein by eating old or tattered webs. But that's not the definitive solution to the mystery. More recent speculation has it that stabilimenta may reflect ultraviolet light and thus lure insects to the web. Whatever the reason for the thick white threads, the argiope is not the only kind of spider that uses them. The orb-weaving *Cyclosus* incorporates them, and so does *Uloborus,* which spins hackled, not sticky, threads to make the bug-catching spiral that connects the radii in its web.

I also see some small commotions at the top edge of the argiope's web. It's not unlucky prey, however, but one, two, three mate-seeking males that pluck at the radii as if they were strumming love songs on a guitar. They're pipsqueaks, one-quarter her size. If one approaches her from behind, she may allow him to crawl over her body before using one of her elegant legs to give him the brush-off. If he doesn't give up but keeps coming back, she may allow him to mate before she uses him for the day's main course; he is, after all, another source of protein. Later, she will hang her large egg sac close to her web. First, she'll extrude a mass of silk; then, suspended below it, she'll lay her eggs upward into the sac. Before she's done, she'll cover the sac with several different types of silk, a process that will command several hours of her short spider life.

Back to work: The tomatoes await me. Bright-Face's arrival in the vines is exciting, but I'll tell only the Chief and Becky's father, Mo, about her. Too many people not only dislike but truly fear spiders with an aboriginal terror that may be genetically programmed as a safety measure, and, frightened, they are quick to smash the soft bodies or spray them with insecticides. It seems perfectly human, which is to say imperfect, to smash and spray without thinking. I marvel that these scaredy-cats grow any plants at all, for all flowers, vegetables, shrubs, fruit and nut trees offer havens to spiders—not just to dozens of argiopes but also to crablike spiny orb weavers, funnel weavers, minuscule orchard spiders with fluorescent orange-red embellishments, and a head-spinning number of harmless others. To be sure, the Point has its venomous arachnids, both the black widow and the brown recluse. I haven't met the latter, but the widow is common and makes herself at home in the hollows of cinder blocks, overturned buckets, and the darkness of our shed and pump house. In spring, when we migrate south, we're careful not to put bare hands in holes and crevices. Nor do I hesitate to spray the pump house before hauling out my crab pots, which are stored for the winter along the back wall. But the argiope, like all her kind, is an object for wonder. We'll try to see that this one does not fall victim to an act of impulsive arachnicide.

The garden is home also to an amazing group of spider lookalikes, the daddy longlegs, which scamper with great agility amid the greenery and scramble, too, along my arms when I pick beans, a task that calls for considerable sitting in one place. They come in a marvelous variety of sizes: The leg tips of some would reach far past the edges of a silver dollar; others would be hard put to cover a dime. The legs are like fine, long suspension cables from which the small, round body hangs. And they're used for much more than just walking—running, sometimes—through the garden's thickets of vegetables and weeds. The legs break easily, allowing daddy longlegs to escape should a predator grab hold. And the second pair of legs actually bears sense organs that convey information about important matters like food and danger.

Though they seem to be spiders, they aren't. Rather, they're members of the arachnid order Opiliones, the "shepherds," and the family Phalangiidae, the "legs" bunch. The reason for "legs" is obvious; that for "shepherds" is vanishing in this increasingly urbanized age. Traditional wisdom has it that the pair of legs second from a daddy longlegs's head will indicate the direction in which a searcher should go in order to find a lost cow. (In my experience, though I haven't looked once for stray cows, one of the second pair of legs is likely to point, say, northeast, while the other aims northwest.) Since the nineteenth century, the British, who once knew them as father longlegs, have called these creatures harvest spiders or harvestmen because they were seen in great numbers at the time of reaping.

How can a creature that closely resembles a spider not *be* a spider? There are a host of differences between the Araneae, or spiderkind, and the Opiliones. One has to do with those legs, which spiders can regenerate but daddy longlegs can't, though the loss of a leg usually does not hinder their ability to scamper at full speed from hither to yon. Another has to do with webs: The spider spins to catch its prey, while the daddy longlegs hunts. And where the spider must paralyze and crush a victim, then suck it dry, the daddy longlegs has jaws that can pull off bits of solid food. Daddy longlegs is also an omnivore, using its first pair of legs to hold such morsels as insects, persimmons, and—in captivity—marshmallows up to its mouth. Water is a necessity as well; a daddy longlegs must take frequent drinks and live in moist places lest its body dry out, a fatal condition. There's a difference, too, in the way that the two arachnids go about sex: The male daddy longlegs has an intromittent penis, while his counterpart in spiderdom uses his legs to insert a sperm package in the female.

Folklore is fascinated by the daddy longlegs. In addition to the creature's reputed ability to locate Bossie, the science writer Sue Hubbell lists other talents. They are eight-legged stars, said to bring good luck to someone who wishes on them. If they walk on your clothes, you'll get new ones. On the negative side they're said to lay their eggs on bats—eggs that hatch out into bedbugs. The basis for this belief is that squashed daddy longlegs and bedbugs both have a somewhat fetid odor. The worst thing of which they're supposedly capable is killing: If one walks on your shoulder, that's it. I am, however, living proof that this is nothing more than idle rumor. As Sue Hubbell writes, the lore is "entertaining but has more to do with us than it does with the biology of daddy longlegs."

Despite the general frisson that they arouse in almost everybody, spiders and daddy longlegs are benign, guardian presences in the garden. They do no harm, not to plants or to persons. The sow bugs are in this league, too, along with the slender little dark brown garden centipedes that look as if they're dancing when they move. Like box turtles, these small animals love the moist, dark place found under leaves—and our garden is usually moist, for we use sprinklers frequently during dry spells. Thin the seedlings or pull a weed— there they are, scurrying away from desiccating sun and wind. Like spiders and daddy longlegs, like grasshoppers and butterflies, centipedes and sow bugs are arthropods, but from that point on they diverge. The centipedes belong to the Myriopoda, the "thousand-leggers." The sow bugs aren't bugs at all but rather crustaceans, of the large order Isopoda, the "equal-leggers," so named for their very short legs that are all the same length. The graceful centipedes in our garden, of the species formally known as *Hemiscolopendra punctiventris*—"point-bellied half-millipede"—have been known seek the shelter of our immobile home in times of drought. Their sudden appearance on the rug or in my cotton throw is enough to occasion a shriek, but they're not to be feared, for they neither bite nor sting. I've never found a sow bug inside. They tend to stay in the garden or under decaying logs in the woods, where they assemble in little groups that tumble over one another like puppies.

As isopods, the sow bugs and their close cousins the pill bugs and sea roaches long ago left most of their relatives behind in the sea and came ashore to lead a landlubber's life. All the terrestrial isopods are also known as wood lice; all have segmented bodies, breathe through gills, and possess seven pairs of leglike appendages. Because wood lice must constantly conserve moisture, they've developed a strategy to stay moist: They do not urinate but instead expel ammonia as a gas. They also recycle their feces: They eat them so that the copper in them doesn't get away—copper is a major component of wood louse blood. And in the world of arthropods wood lice are the opossums: The females brood their eggs in a fluid-filled marsupium—a pouch—in the mother's body; these terrestrial cousins of shrimp and barnacles have brought the sea ashore for purposes of raising their young. The hatchlings stay in the pouch until they're big enough to fend for themselves; on emergence they look like tiny adults, and it will take them a year of successive molts to attain full size.

Sea roaches, also known as beach slaters and boat bugs, are formally known as *Ligia exotica;* the genus refers to Ligeia—"shrill voice"—one of the Greek sirens who tried to lure Odysseus to his death, while the species name means "foreign." They are silent, however, not shrill voiced. I mention them not because they're in our garden but rather because we see them by the hundreds as they scamper swiftly along the top and sides of our seawall and the pilings of our pier, from which they occasionally descend to wet their whistles —their gills—in the river. The local mallards run along the seawalls at the Point snatching and gobbling up sea roaches with the greatest zest. The pill bugs are identified by their trick of being able to curl up into a slick, smooth ball to protect themselves from disturbance and from being eaten by predators. Their family is that of the Armadillidae, in recognition of their armadillolike ability to turn themselves into a plated sphere. Pill bugs are not abundant in our garden. Far more sow bugs—thousands on tumbling thousands more—are at home there throughout the summer. Their formal name is *Porcellio laevis,* the "smooth [or hairless] sowbug." *Porcellio* may also mean "little sow"; because of the animals' gentle and companionable inclination to group closely together, it's easy to see a litter of fat, nuzzling little pigs. The female sow bug is something of an Amazon, for she's able to reproduce parthenogenically. By this method, however, she will bear only female offspring; the cooperation of a male is needed to produce the opposite sex. He will fertilize her by using a pair of his legs to transfer his sperm.

The New World was not the original habitat of sow and pill bugs. How did they get here? As it happens, they're fellow travelers, or synanthropes, that often accompany people moving from hither to yon. The earliest fossils of terrestrial isopods, found in Baltic amber, date back thirty-five to forty million years ago. They so closely resemble contemporary forms that it can safely be assumed that their ancestors left the sea in a far more distant time. Worldwide there are five thousand species of wood lice. Those that inhabit the Americas almost certainly sailed across the ocean with the European explorers and colonists, and research on pill bugs shows that species found in the northeastern United States are genetically akin to species living in Britain and northern Europe, while species found in the Southwest are remarkably similar to those that inhabit southern Europe. As go the Pilgrims or conquistadores, so go the wood lice.

The brown stink bug, officially christened *Euschistus servus*, the "slavish or servile well-split bug," was here to begin with. It was given its scientific moniker by Thomas Say (1787–1843), who published the monumental three-volume *American Entomology* in the 1820s. He was much honored in the world of biology; his name was given to *Sayornis*, Say's bird, the avian genus that includes the eastern phoebe and Say's phoebe. (The latter is *Sayornis saya*—"Say's Say's bird.") The only resemblance that the brown stink bug has to a bird is that both have wings. It is an insect, a true bug, belonging to the order Hemiptera, the "half-wings." Stink bugs come in many versions—the brown, green, and southern green among them—and all bear a triangular shield, the scutellum, in the center of their backs; it may have been this shield to which Say referred when he came up with the designation *well-split*. The brown version can be distinguished from the others by its dull brown color and the easy-to-see checkered border beneath its wing covers. It's particularly abundant on our beans and tomatoes, where it dines upon leaves and fruits. Its preadult nymphs are also predatory carnivores that suck the juices out of creatures like millipedes. But the bug is not so rapacious that I feel compelled to spray or dust it. There's enough here for both humankind and stink bugs. The common name refers to the unpleasantly strong, sourish odor that the creature emits when it is disturbed. I have been told that some people are able to sniff it out on the plants over which a stink bug has traveled, but my nose is deficient, able to detect only the grossest kinds of stench, and the bug announces its presence by letting me see it.

The brown stink bug is part of a large family, the Pentatomidae, the "five-sectioned bugs," about which Jean Henri Fabre, the French naturalist, has written an admiring tale. Observing the stink bugs in his garden, his curiosity unflagging, he notes that members of the family lay their eggs in neat, closely packed ranks on the undersides of leaves. "What a delightful collection of miniature vases in translucent alabaster, barely clouded with light grey!" he exclaims, and calls them "masterpieces of elegant simplicity." The eggs are the insect equivalent of jewel boxes: little barrel-shaped containers, each embellished with symmetrically placed spots and lines and a flat lid that opens neatly when the young bugs hatch.

I find stink bugs intriguing for another reason: They use the plants in the garden as if the greenery were telephone wires or, these days, fiber-optic cable. They send their communications by way of stems and leaves. They're not the only animals that use this system; many other insects like lacewings and katydids, along with spiders, frogs, and lizards, transmit vibrations—songs—over the green telegraph. Sonograms show a wide variety of sounds, and it's possible for people to hear them, too, if they are picked up by a vibrational microphone; the song of one courting thornbug has been described as "a rich, bubbling down-sweep of tone and percussion that courses through the plant." The songs contain various sorts of messages, from offspring summoning their mother to defend them to a male advertising for a mate. In one experiment male and female stink bugs were placed on a many-stemmed ivy. The male bugs, arriving at a branch, would place a set of legs on one stem and another set on the other stem. It appears that this bipartite arrangement enables better reception of a female's song and also indicates the direction in which she may be found.

As I pick the garden's bounty, I imagine a mysterious plantborne music beyond the range of hearing—burbles and clicks and percussive drumbeats. The green telegraph—all the more reason to share the garden with its denizens: dark field crickets, mole crickets that tunnel through the earth, grasshoppers spitting brown juice when I catch them, dragonflies—eight-spotted skimmers and shining green darners—perched on the tops of tomato cages, twiglike walkingsticks, brown Chinese mantises, humpbacked buffalo treehoppers with large dark red eyes, leaffooted bugs wearing flattened wings on their hind legs, broccoli-loving harlequin bugs wearing a motley of black and bright orange, steely gray assassin bugs that feed on the larvae of plant-eating insects, and a host of beetles, including cheerfully red six-spotted ladybugs, huge eastern Hercules beetles plodding along like tiny tanks, and the little bean leaf beetles, yellow with brown polka dots and possessed of an appetite twice as big as they are. Only a few of the garden's arthropods trigger my urge to exterminate. In every case, my choice lies between deciding whether a plant will produce people food or food for insects. Luckily, some of the villains are not abundant; rarely do we suffer serious depredations from the motor-jaws of the tomato and tobacco hornworms found on our tomato vines (both kinds of hornworms indiscriminately infest the members of the nightshade family, including horseradish). Nor have Japanese beetles ever caused much bother, though on occasion I've caught them dining on tender young eggplant leaves. Striped blister beetles can be found on the tomatoes at the end of the season, but by that time we've harvested enough to see us through the winter. There are just two insects that we regularly war against— the Colorado potato beetle and the cabbageworm. Both work all manner of depredations, minor to devastating, as they follow the dictates encoded in their genes.

Though the Chief and I don't grow spuds, and North Carolina is a far piece from the montane West, that beetle is here in full force. Dubbed *Leptinotarsa decemlineata*, the "ten-lined skinny-legger," by the nomenclators, it feasts on eggplant and bean leaves and on the beans themselves. Both the brown-and-yellow-striped adults and the plump, squishy orange nymphs are insatiable; between them, they can strip the young leaves from eggplants overnight. I've also found them in both stages on tomato vines. Until the 1800s the species was indeed confined to the Rocky Mountains, where it lived in meadows on the lower slopes and subsisted on members of the Solanaceae, the nightshades. That's the family to which potatoes, peppers, and eggplants belong, along with herbs like black nightshade, henbane, and belladonna. Somehow—I suspect through un-witting human agency, people who collected plants not knowing what was stowed within the leaves—the beetle was transported out of its original home. It proceeded to spread all over the country. It also crossed the Atlantic and now infests Europe. Their damage to our beans is minor, and I can squash them as I pick. But they can wreak major devastation on our mad-apples when the tender seed-lings are first put in the ground. For the first few weeks I dust the plants with Sevin: End of problem. As fortune has it, the eggplant toughens as the plant matures and ceases to be of culinary interest to Colorado potato beetles long before it sets its fruit.

I've already mentioned the Bt treatment that we administer to the larvae of the cabbage butterflies. I've seen other treatments sug-gested, such as dusting the plants with a mixture of flour and salt, and spraying them with sour milk or an infusion of garlic. And Pliny offers two surefire ways of exterminating caterpillars: placing the skull of a horse on a fence post or hanging a river crab in the middle of the garden. Where we'd find a horse's skull, I don't know, but we do have plenty of crabs in the river. Nonetheless, we head without hesitation for the Bt, for it is sure to protect our small crop. Those ravening, soft-bodied cabbageworms, new-leaf green with a narrow lemon-colored dorsal stripe, will gnaw gaping holes in any of the coles—cabbage, broccoli, cauliflower, and the rest—if given half a chance. Their appetites zero in on the mustard oil glycosides found in the leaves of all the Cruciferae, generally toxic compounds that kill other insects. These oils, rightly blamed for the sulfurous smell of cooking cabbage, were used to manufacture mustard gas in World War I and are employed today as emetics. But just as tobacco hornworms are immune to nicotine poisoning as they chow down, so are cabbageworms completely resistant to the toxins in their favorite foods. The creatures are not indigenous to the New World but rather came here by accident in the 1860s, when they arrived in Canada—unwitting human agency at work again. They were first noticed near Montréal and have since spread merrily throughout North America. The insect, no slouch at reproduction, is capable of producing three generations a year in Canada, more farther south. I watch the butterflies fluttering delicately above the green leaves on which they'll lay their eggs. They're the picture of innocence—wings a bridal white adorned with beauty spots of sooty black. And their name, *Pieris rapae,* invokes a time before time when the Muses, also called the Pierides, found inspiration for their dances and songs as they lingered beside the sweet, cool waters of the Pierian Spring in southwest Macedonia. Combined with the butterfly's species name, *rapae,* the whole binomial translates as "muse of the turnip." Not so odd, when you consider that turnips share their genus, *Brassica,* with *B. oleracea,* the grand host of cabbages and their kin; *B. chinensis,* Chinese cabbage; *B. juncea,* mustard; *B. napobrassica,* rutabaga; and many edible others. But we like cabbages as well as they do, and being large and merciless, we do them in.

There's one uninvited guest in our garden about which we can do nothing—except to watch where we step. It's *Solenopsis invicta*—the "unconquered or unconquerable grooved-face," more commonly called the red imported fire ant. It's a small reddish creature, but it shows its fire not in its color but with its sting. This tiny insect, not much bigger than a caraway seed, bites first, then injects venom with the sharp precision instrument located at its nether end. And there's never just one ant inflicting damage, no; as many as five hundred thousand workers may inhabit one mound. As soon as they are disturbed by a stick, a foot, or the legs of my sit-upon, a dark mass of them, savage as any Mongol horde, boils upward and attacks. A determined swarm savages the unwary victim, marching in quick step right up your pant leg to your crotch. It does no good to try to brush them off, for that is tantamount to asking them to sting your hands and arms. The result of the invasion: a host of small blisters that itch most horridly and end in pus-filled, necrotic sores that take nigh onto forever to heal.

Red fire ants have not been with us always. Native to western Brazil and Paraguay, they arrived in the United States around 1930 as stowaways, probably in the soil around the roots of imported plants. A related species, the imported black fire ant, entered the country earlier, around 1919 in the port of Mobile, but it has not spread out of Alabama and Mississippi. *S. invicta,* though, has conquered the South and is heading west into Arizona. It's possible to slow their advance with pesticides, but nothing that we know of can truly contain or exterminate them. And if a colony is bothered overmuch, it simply picks up and moves to a more peaceful location. Red fire ants have become a fact of life.

They're certainly a fact in our garden. Overnight a mound will rise up like a small Vesuvius and be just as ready to erupt, pouring forth a fiery stream of ants the instant that they're jostled. It behooves us to keep an eye out for those low constructions at the base of a bean plant, on the side of a hill of butternuts, in the middle of a path between the rows. And the mounds can be distinguished from those of harmless ants because they have many door holes in the earth rather than a single opening. Over the years, bumping into fire ants in the garden or standing on them accidentally while looking skyward at birds, I've been stung and stung again—so often, indeed, that I've been inoculated. The stings are painful, yes, but the blisters and necrosis no longer develop. The Chief has wisely avoided taking the same step to defend his flesh against fire ants.

What an intricate community our garden is—food plants side by side with weeds, turtles keeping company with rabbits and green snakes, and the whole works filled with arthropods feeding, breeding, singing their songs. High-striding runners, elegant spinners, loopers and leapers, high fliers, and all the moiling rest of them— for the first time, I actually envision Queen Mab's waggon. Wheels a-whirl, coachmen cracking their whips, it races through the garden when I'm not looking. I'd only read about it before, in the first act of *Romeo and Juliet,* where Mercutio, describing it in great detail, castigates his friend Romeo for showing true madness in the matter of love:

> O! then, I see, Queen Mab hath been with you. . . .
> She is the fairies' midwife, and she comes
> In shape no bigger than an agate stone
> On the forefinger of an alderman,
> Drawn with a team of little atomies
> Athwart men's noses as they lie asleep:
> Her waggon-spokes made of long spinners' legs;
> The cover, of the wings of grasshoppers;
> The traces, of the smallest spider's web;
> The collars, of the moonshine's watery beam;
> Her whip, of cricket's bone; the lash, of film;
> Her waggoner, a small grey-coated gnat,
> Not half so big as a round little worm
> Pricked from the lazy finger of a maid;

Her chariot is an empty hazelnut,
Made by the joiner squirrel or old grub,
Time out of mind the fairies' coach-makers,
And in this state she gallops night by night
Through lovers' brains, and then they dream of love.

And not just love: Mab puts dreams of fees into the heads of snoring lawyers, and sneaks kisses into the nighttime visions of wrinkled old ladies. She addles the brains of the men and women whose overweening lusts and greeds invite her to invade their innermost desirings.

The garden houses almost every part that's needed for her careering waggon—the whips and webs and grasshopper wings. The only item that it can't provide is the body of her chariot: Hazelnuts do not grow at Great Neck Point. But go around the corner from our garden and you'll find wild pignuts and tame pecans, either of which would suit the fairies' midwife quite well. Here it does not seem that she's midwife only to the fairies; she's keeper of all the world's arthropods. She needs them, for the garden is her stable and those that live amid the plants are her suppliers.

And I find that Mab is running wild. Her waggon races through my head. She brings me visions—shimmering mirages—of a perfect garden, one in which all lives, both plant and animal, are conducted in the greatest harmony. The potato beetles munch only upon the plants with leaves to spare. The weeds are polite, giving ample room to those less brash and aggressive.

I must be mad.

A BLOOMING
OF GARDENERS

THE SOIL OF GREAT NECK POINT grows vegetable gardeners as readily as it does vegetables. And they tend toward eccentricity. To begin with, their gardens cover the extremes from absolutely messy to preternaturally tidy. On the one hand, there's the wildly overgrown, minimally productive plot put in by the keeper of the ever-crowing cock, and on the other, a fenced and gated garden so free of weeds that, as one of the neighbors has surmised, it could have been created only by someone who was potty-trained at pistol point. Several of the gardens enchant me. Let me take you on a tour and introduce you not only to the gardens but also to the people who've designed and tended them.

Vegetables, Milkweed, and Popcorn Trees:
DOROTHY'S GARDEN

WHEN I CALL Dorothy to make sure of the ingredients for her most excellent green tomato casserole, she asks, "What do you know about monarch butterflies?"

"Only a little," I say.

The problem is, the monarch caterpillars that she rescued from the wasps are dying. Last year the wasps killed every last one that was dining on her milkweed plants. Then summer tanagers, the brownish yellow females and the rosy red males, proceeded to feast upon the wasps, but this year, for the first time in Dorothy's thirty-year-long acquaintance with the Point, the tanagers have not appeared. Trouble in their tropical wintering range? Destruction of habitat, thanks to raging development on their breeding grounds at the Point and its vicinity? We do not know. Only the mockingbird repeats their call. In the sad absence of tanagers, in order to save the caterpillars from hungry and therefore murderous wasps, she took them off the milkweed plants in her garden, brought them into the house, and put them in an aquarium with plenty of milkweed leaves to eat. Two formed chrysalises, one of which turned mortally black, while the other caterpillars did not have the chance to pupate before death struck. I cannot tell her the reason for this year's mortality, but I do know that the survival rate, egg to butterfly, is minuscule. Like fish and frogs, they lay great quantities of eggs, but only one in a thousand will ever mature into a reproducing adult.

Her garden features milkweed strictly to entice the monarchs: *Danaus plexippus,* the "horse-driving Danaus." The genus name honors the brother of the mythical Aegyptos, whose name is borne today in the English-speaking world by the country on the Nile; Danaus himself fathered fifty daughters, who—with one exception— slew their Egyptian husbands on their wedding nights. The myth is grisly; the butterfly is not. As for *horse-driving,* it's an epithet that Homer bestowed upon heroes; I surmise that the nomenclator either wished to honor the ancient bard or chose the name—this is a long shot—to acknowledge the butterfly's remarkable migrations. What an amazing creature the monarch is—fragility married to extreme endurance! Its eastern populations in the United States and southern Canada migrate from their summertime ranges to winter in Mexico; there they haunt the forests of oyamel firs and hang from the trees like living flames. (Monarchs that summer west of the Rockies spend the winter along the coast of California.) In spring the butterflies return—not the same butterflies that flew south, but those of later generations that hatched out on the way back north. It's a rough journey; I've seen some with tatters in their black-and-orange wings. Why do they alone, of all the world's butterflies, migrate? The answer seems to be that monarchs originated in the Tropics of South America and, over evolutionary time, gradually made their way north to take advantage of abundant stands of milkweed—but being tropical creatures, they never developed hibernating mechanisms for coping with cold weather and cannot tolerate temperatures below freezing. If their kind is to survive, it must make an annual flight away from death by hypothermia.

The springtime monarchs that find Great Neck Point zero in on Dorothy's milkweed, a tall, showy sort with huge and fragrant purple-red flower clusters. It's not usual to find milkweed in an otherwise immaculately tended garden, and I ask Dorothy how it comes to be there. With monarch butterflies in mind, she gathered seeds while on vacation in Utah, planted them on the Carolina coast, and waited. In her first few tries nothing whatsoever sprouted. Then she realized that the western soil in which the parent plants grew is highly alkaline; she adjusted her soil's pH accordingly. Behold: *Asclepias syriaca* rose and thrived. The genus of the milkweeds honors the Greek god of medicine, while the species name of common milkweed—"from

Syria"—misleads, for the plant is native to the New World. Its brown seeds attached to the pods by silky threads especially fascinated Henry David Thoreau, who describes at length the bursting of the pods and the seeds released to sail off on the breeze. "I do not see but the seeds which are ripened in New England may plant themselves in Pennsylvania," he writes. "I am interested in the fate or success of every such venture that autumn sends forth. And for this end these silken streamers have been perfected themselves all summer, snugly packed in this light chest, a perfect adaptation to this end—a prophecy not only of the fall, but of future springs."

In an unobtrusive way milkweed is a useful plant. Folk medicine has stewed its roots to make potions that alleviate asthma, coughing, and pain; its young sprouts can be cooked and eaten like asparagus, its seeds with their streamers have been used like kapok to stuff pillows and life jackets, and its milky sap, containing latex, can be induced to make rubber. The sap also protects the butterflies and their larvae, creatures that are elegantly striped in orange and black outlined with white. Chowing down on the leaves, the caterpillars ingest the sap, which contains powerful cardiac glycosides, produced by special metabolic processes in the plant (digitalis, from foxglove, is the most familiar of these substances). Their food thus gives the caterpillars a bitter flavor that is not only disagreeable but also toxic to birds; birds that have eaten monarchs in any stage have been observed to suffer nausea and outright vomiting for up to half an hour after they've consumed such prey. Wasps, however, seem to be immune. Dorothy watched last year as wasps bent over the caterpillars, seized them, and squeezed out their juices till they were light enough to carry away.

Dorothy, petite, graying, and bursting at the seams with energy, came to Great Neck Point via the Marine Corps. She was born in

Colorado, where her father raised sugar beets. Her husband, Kent, is a retired colonel of Marines. When he served at Cherry Point Marine Air Station, only twenty miles from our peninsula, they bought a waterfront lot, where they camped for years, while their two daughters were growing up, in an Air Stream travel trailer. When Kent retired, the Air Stream was also retired, except for a short spell as living quarters while they built their slate-foundation, cedar-siding house, an elegant dwelling with great glass doors and windows facing the wide and salty Neuse. And they built it with their own two hands, plus the hands of any neighbors who wanted to saw a board or pound in nails. Like us, Dorothy and Kent have acquired land from the original farming family, and their lot now stretches between river and dirt road. Kent has turned part of this large yard into a putting green.

As the house was built, landscaping was made part and parcel of the construction: a live oak sapling transplanted from the woods, a box elder that had volunteered elsewhere planted in the backyard, a garden of azaleas along with a delicate Japanese maple installed in a sinuous bed over the septic tank. A weathered wooden wheelbarrow holding potted plants serves as a movable garden, now stationed here, now there, in the fashion of the emperor Tiberius's mobile cucumber beds in the first century A.D. Amid the lush hostas of the foundation planting sits a Japanese lantern carved of stone; it is an enduring souvenir of the years that Kent, Dorothy with him, spent in Okinawa with the Marines. Bluebird boxes have been set on posts, front yard and back, and a split-rail fence, decked with coral honeysuckle that attracts hummingbirds and orchard orioles, separates lawn from dirt road. Dorothy is a bird person, keen at spotting well-hidden nests and evanescent transients like the little sandpipers. And with such space, vegetables were and are a necessity. Dorothy laid out her garden in the last of the Air Stream days, with its five thirty-foot-long raised beds and protective fence: peas on a trellis, broccoli, green beans, onions, carrots, long slender burpless Japanese cucumbers, slicing tomatoes of several varieties, and plum tomatoes. It's a Jeffersonian garden, with something always coming to perfection. I envy Dorothy her tomatoes—they produce till October while ours are done at the end of July. To our good fortune, she doles out her sweet bounty liberally to the needy.

And milkweed, a towering and sturdy specimen with huge blooms, stands like a sentinel amid the vegetables. Fertilizer, meant for the edibles, does wonders also for a wild plant. It's not the only flower in the garden. Small poppies raise ferny leaves and golden blossoms beside the onion and tomato beds. Bachelor's buttons with flowers as blue as a summer sky rise three feet tall along the fence that also holds the garden gate. (No roaming dogs will chase rabbits through this garden, thank you, leaving a devastation of broken stems and crushed fruit in their wake.) Gaillardia is also there, big pinwheel blooms of yellow and maroon. And in the southeast quadrant, catty-corner from the gate, popcorn trees volunteer with great enthusiasm every year. Their parent stands just outside the fence.

Popcorn tree—some call it the tallow tree. It came from China to South Carolina in the 1700s and has since snuggled in from North Carolina to Texas along the southeastern Atlantic seaboard and the Gulf Coast. Botanists know it as *Sapium sebiferum,* the "resinous, tallow-bearing tree." A member of the Euphorbiaceae or spurge family, it shares its genus with one of the small tropical trees—there are several—that give the world Mexican jumping beans (the jumper is a moth caterpillar that responds to the warmth

of a hand but also wriggles anyway as it gnaws the pulp in the trees'
beanlike seeds). Though the tallow tree does not yield resin like a
pine, its leaf stems exude a sticky substance; its milky sap is poisonous. And its seeds are covered with vegetable tallow, chemically the
equivalent of animal suet; it forms a waxy coating that the Chinese
—and anyone else who is so inclined—may boil off for making soap
and candles. In the early 1900s the U.S. Department of Agriculture
encouraged its planting in Gulf Coast states as a means of starting a
soap industry, which (unlike the tree) never got off the ground.
Those seeds are the tree's popcorn; when the fruit ripens fully, it
explodes, exposing white seeds in a curled-back brown hull just like
something produced by Orville Redenbacher. But they are one of
nature's outbursts, not something puffed up on a kitchen stove. In
fall the densely clustered leaves glow red as embers. Till recently,
when she learned to identify the infant trees by their first true leaves,
Dorothy thought that they were weeds and wielded a stern, extrac-
tive hand. Now she gives them away. Fast growing, gloriously leafy,
the tallow tree is not only attractive but also able to tolerate both full
sun and full shade. Nurseries sell it as an ornamental species. But
Dorothy might do better to keep thinking of it as a weed. Left to its
own devices, the tree is quick to clone, sending up replicas from its
roots until it is surrounded by an impenetrable thicket of trees
exactly like itself. Since its introduction by the USDA it has accomplished a land grab of considerable proportions in the coastal
prairies of eastern Texas. Reaching maturity in only three years, it
also spreads itself by way of its popcorn, which birds eat eagerly and
then disperse. And the tree's fallen leaves contain chemicals that
alter soil chemistry and so deter or prevent the growth of native vegetation. For these many reasons, *S. sebiferum* has earned a place on

The Nature Conservancy's list of the dozen species of plants and animals least wanted in America. Dorothy, happily, is able to keep her one tree under control.

Feast for the eyes, feast for the body—Dorothy's garden is both. Its colors, flavors, textures, shapes, and movements are kaleidoscopic, changing as the seasons turn. It entertains yellow-rumped and palm warblers, purple finches, chipping sparrows, bluebirds, killdeer, and mockingbirds. Not only monarch caterpillars find food for metamorphosis amid the vegetables; black swallowtail larvae, striped green and black with golden polka dots, may also be found there munching on the feathery leaves of carrots. As I walk past, I always linger to see the latest act in the great garden show. Often Dorothy is there, sharing the good earth's succulence and the ways in which she likes to prepare it.

Here are two of the recipes in which she trusts.

What the Hell Green Tomato Casserole

FRIED GREEN TOMATOES are famous, thanks to Fannie Flagg, that quintessential southern belle (which is to say, a charming ding-a-ling). And where would my meat loaf be without green tomato pickle, made according to my grandmother's recipe from unripe fruits just after frost kills the vines? Sometimes I gather green fruits before a frost, or take them from vines attacked by wilt, and jump the gun on making pickle. Dorothy offers still a third way of turning green tomatoes, large and small, into a delectable accompaniment to any supper, whether it features hamburgers or filet mignon. She learned it originally from TV chef Justin Wilson's program on the Public Broadcasting System. I confess to having gussied up the recipe with a little butter, but those averse to cholesterol can omit it. I've also gussied it down, omitting the Hell—the Tabasco sauce, that is—if children are expected to partake.

This recipe is made by eye, not quantities of ingredients. Select a baking dish, small or large depending on the appetites at hand, and pick enough tomatoes to fill it. Italian bread crumbs may be used; I prefer, however, to muddle up my own seasoned crumbs, using a sprinkling of garlic powder and Parmesan cheese, along with fresh oregano in summer or the dried, homegrown kind in winter.

INGREDIENTS
green tomatoes, sliced thin
Vidalia onions, sliced thin
butter
Tabasco sauce
Romano cheese
paprika
salt
Italian bread crumbs

PREHEAT the oven to 325 degrees.

LIGHTLY OIL an ovenproof baking dish. Add vegetables, beginning with a layer of tomatoes. Add a layer of onions. Place thin pats of butter on these ingredients. Add two dashes of Tabasco to each layer of tomatoes and onions. Sprinkle with Romano, paprika, and salt, lightly or heavily according to taste. Top with seasoned bread crumbs. For a shallow dish, one layer will do; for a deeper dish, make two or three.

BAKE for 1 hour, or until the onions are done.

Peruvian Sauce

DOROTHY ALSO OFFERS a recipe for a sweet, slightly tangy relish made of ripe tomatoes, along with homegrown onions, bell peppers, and one hot pepper. She learned it from the neighbor immediately upriver—a man who cooks and cans up a storm. He also grows the hot peppers not found in Dorothy's vegetable patch. And he found the recipe in a now-superannuated booklet of recipes put out by the Ball Corporation, maker of Mason jars. This heirloom concoction, not found in modern cookbooks, gives real zest to ordinary fare like hamburgers, meat loaf, and hot dogs.

INGREDIENTS

4 quarts red-ripe tomatoes, peeled, cored and
   chopped (about 24)

1 quart chopped onions

1 quart pared, cored, and chopped apples

1½ cups chopped green bell peppers
   (about 3 medium peppers)

1 hot red pepper, seeded and finely diced

1 clove garlic, crushed

3 cups brown sugar, packed

1 tablespoon salt

1 tablespoon ground allspice

1 teaspoon ground cinnamon

3 cups vinegar

COMBINE the tomatoes, onions, apples, peppers, garlic, and sugar. Cook slowly until thick, about 1 hour. As the mixture thickens, stir frequently to prevent sticking.

ADD the salt, spices, and vinegar. Cook until as thick as you want it, 45 to 60 minutes.

POUR, boiling hot, into hot canning jars, leaving ⅛ inch of headroom. Adjust the caps. Process in a water bath for 15 minutes.

MAKES about 6 pints

Vegetables Under the Oaks: TOM'S GARDEN

WHEN I ARRIVE at Tom and Kathleen's barn-red cottage on a sticky-hot summer Sunday and park in the shade of a large oak, Kathleen comes outside to welcome me. Tom's inside picking out crabs. A bucket containing at least two dozen large, well-packed jimmies sits on the kitchen table and, beside it, a bowl already half filled with meat. He sets his own crab pots in the river, which flows a mere fifty feet from a screened-in front porch that's almost as big as the cottage itself. The air-conditioning feels paradisical. But the garden calls us both outside.

I've heard considerable about it from Dorothy and Becky, who shake their heads with incredulous admiration as they speak of it. Dorothy says, "Believe it or not, he actually grows things in the *shade.*"

The Chief and I have known Tom and his family for all of our days at the Point. He and Kathleen have lived at river's edge since 1977. Their first son was born four years later—he's now in college —and a second son joined them in 1986. Early on the family supplied the neighborhood with friendly black Labs that swam in the river and came to visit all and sundry. And it's Tom, a small brisk man with a floor-covering business in town, who installs carpets for the Point and puts down vinyl for our kitchens and baths. Kathleen works as a computer specialist, keeping the Unix system up and running at the Cherry Point Marine Corps Air Station's depot for repairing military aircraft. In the years that they've been our neighbors we've seen his hair go from dark brown to salt and pepper, while Kathleen's has turned silver, contrasting beautifully with her tan, round-cheeked face. Both are given to smiling much and merrily.

The garden, a fenced rectangular plot, lies only thirty feet from the house and is adjacent to the dirt road giving access to Tom's part of the Point, around the corner and downriver from ours. The garden is indeed shaded; it's almost crepuscular. Several white oaks with trunks a foot in diameter, two sturdy, thick-leaved American hollies, an old peach tree, a generously spreading fig, and a small stand of pines cast almost perpetual shadow over the entire enterprise. Cut them down? Never! Tom likes trees. I note a small gap in the canopy, though, that allows a patch of sunlight about the size of a baby's blanket to travel as the day wears on; it rests for the moment on a sprawl of cherry tomatoes. But there's an advantage to a garden in the shade: It produces into October, November, well after gardens in the sun have been burned out. And it's been there under the oaks for a good fifteen years.

"Oddly, the place where I grow vegetables is no-man's-land," he says. "No one owns it." This peculiar state of affairs came about when an early resident sold off a small chunk of acreage and the surveys somehow ignored the small piece wedged between the road and the yards of Tom and the neighbor who lives immediately upriver. Both of them use it for growing things, she putting in flower beds and he, vegetables. And everywhere there are leaves, fruit, colors. Plants really do grow here in the shadows. 'Better Boy' tomatoes stand in cages near the prostrate cherry tomatoes. Two fences inside the garden now support the drying remains of 'Blue Lake' pole beans. I mention that we grow the bush variety of 'Blue Lake', but Tom says he's never had any luck with that. Earlier in the season the fences gave peas something to scale in their thrust toward the light, and the peas then gave Tom and Kathleen a fair crop. In one row kale leaves rise dark green and crinkly; in another a leftover from the spring cauliflower patch has bolted, sending up a mast of small yellow flowers. Over in a corner near the dirt road parsley that's going to seed rises tall. Underfoot—"Go ahead, all right to walk on it," Tom says—is a thick, living carpet of New Zealand spinach, which is not a true spinach but rather a kind of green that tastes like spinach when it's cooked and, better, does not bolt and is also able to withstand the summer heat that does in the real thing. Native to New Zealand, it was brought to the world in the 1770s by Captain James Cook. These greens, lush and inviting, are volunteers. Tom allows that spinach is one of his all-time favorites—"But I only get a decent crop every five years." Lacking anything else, these plants from Down Under will do. And in the shadows colors glow—lambent green, radiant yellow, red-hot red: hot and sweet banana peppers, pencil-thin cayennes, serrano chilies, plump little jalapeños. It looks as if Tom is as fond of fiery capsicum as he is of spinach. It may be that Tom's hot peppers have more capsaicin than most, for the harder they must fight for their lives in less-than-ideal conditions, the more heat they develop.

Nor are these vegetables all that he grows. The patch has given rise to such sweet edibles as carrots and such (to me) tasteless stuff as summer squashes. In late winter and earliest spring, when the oaks (if not the hollies and pines) are leafless and a bit of sunshine can cast cool light upon much of the garden, Tom sets in broccoli, leeks, and scallions, as well as cauliflower. He uses no commercial fertilizer and sprays on insecticides only in cases of dire emergency. But he does fertilize his crops. He sets crab pots in the river, and every other day in summer he picks out their cooked meat; afterward, the crab shells and legs are worked into the garden, along with the shells and heads from any shrimp the family has eaten. These remains break down very quickly. Tom believes that these gifts from the sea provide the superior nutrients that a garden in the shade requires. Hearing this, I'm sure that he knows Pan and old Silvanus. He's fully in touch with the numinous forces of soil and seed.

How did Tom come to vegetable gardening, which obviously delights his soul? The projects in Queens, New York, where he grew up as one of nine children in an Irish Catholic family, are not conducive to an urge to touch earth. He explains that he caught growing fever as a boy, when he visited an uncle who lived and farmed in New Hampshire. "His plants were huge. Or maybe they just looked that way because I was a small guy back then," Tom says. "But that was the beginning. Now I plant but I have no time to tend things. Can't wait to get out of that carpet store so I can just go and garden."

We go inside. Tom resumes picking out crabs, and the three of us talk. I ask if Tom has ever used horizontal wires laced up and down with twine as a support for his pole beans. He's tried that method but prefers fencing. Kathleen says, "And he's never paid for any of it, not the fence for the beans, not the fence around the garden. He has an eye for the road. How many bungee cords do you find along the road each month, Tom?"

"At least five," he says. Since he's lived here he's been a one-man cleanup crew along the twelve miles of farm-to-market road that has long connected the Point with the highway into town. In this rural area, which long lacked any trash services except for do-it-yourself

Dumpster bins, people often disposed of things worn out or unwanted in any location—in the woods, along the road, in the river. Tom began tidying his route to town long before the Adopt-a-Highway movement came into being, and he collected treasures like aluminum cans, bungee cords, and fencing along with the trash.

The talk turns to food. I ask for recipes that use vegetables grown under oaks. "We don't go in for fast food," Kathleen says. "No Hamburger Helper, nothing like that. We always make spaghetti sauce from scratch." The sauce, however, cannot be replicated by any recipe, for it tends to include all the leftovers—carrots, beans, zucchini—lingering in the refrigerator. But each of them offers a particular shady recipe. And before I leave Tom ducks out to the garden again and gathers a right smart batch of pungent peppers for me to take home.

Fried Zucchini: Kathleen's Choice

GIVEN THE ABUNDANCE with which, willy-nilly, summer squashes form and mature, it never hurts to have more than one recipe on hand. Sliced and served raw, they add color to salads. Cooked, they appear in many incarnations—soups, purees, pickles, ratatouilles, and even pizza toppings—that depend on seasonings for flavor. Kathleen vows that this simple recipe for preparing zucchini or any other summer squash is a crowd pleaser, a dish agreeable to adults and children alike. "It looks a fright," she says of the cooking process. "The breading comes off when you turn it, but keep turning." Fright or not, it has led me to put my general negativity about summer squash on hold and frizzle up a batch. (Sometimes, when neighbors' crops produce exponentially, it's better to receive with grace than to say No.)

INGREDIENTS

summer squash,
    enough for the number of appetites to be satisfied
water
flour, bread crumbs, or a mixture of both
salt and pepper to taste
oil

SLICE squash into ¼-inch rounds or chunks. Dip in water.

PUT FLOUR, bread crumbs, or mixed flour and crumbs into a paper bag. Season with salt and pepper. Add the moistened squash and shake till it is thoroughly coated.

COVER THE BOTTOM of a skillet with oil and heat till the oil looks hot and shimmery. Add the squash. Turn and keep turning till the squash is soft. Serve.

Bananas Peppers with Onions: Tom's Favorite

"THIS IS GREAT with hamburgers, hot dogs, steak, sausage, any kind of meat sandwich," says Tom, who eats hot peppers raw or cooked with almost every meal. When I ask what kind of banana pepper he prefers, sweet or hot, he shrugs. "Depends on what I pick." Kathleen adds, "It's always a surprise."

Tom suggests cutting the peppers and onions into the longest, thinnest strips possible. Again, as with many recipes for using produce from a home garden, measurements are made by eye. Judge by the number of people who'd like to load their hamburgers or steak with it. If, by some remote chance, there are leftovers, they can be refrigerated and reheated.

INGREDIENTS

banana peppers

onions

olive oil

SLICE peppers lengthwise into long, thin strips. Slice onions into the longest strips possible.

COVER the bottom of a skillet with olive oil and heat it. Sauté the pepper and onion strips till the onion is soft and translucent.

DEVOUR!

Deviation Amid the Vegetables:
BECKY AND DENNIS'S GARDEN

"WE'RE GOING TO make a bird," Dennis says. He's digging as energetically as a puppy burying a bone, into a huge heap of sandy clay. The objective: to fashion a mold. Early July, the day is sweltering; sweat rolls off his face, drips off his short, grizzled beard, and splashes earthward in great drops. Two smoke-gray kittens gambol around the base of the clay heap, and a ferret named Snarf ducks in and out of the holes already dug in the clay. Behind Dennis, a small, rust-speckled electric cement mixer spins slowly around to stir together the bird's ingredients—a mixture of sand, peat moss, Portland cement, and a slosh of water. Dennis calls this thick glop "bioconcrete" because of the organic peat moss. He found the recipe in a catalog that advertised molds for making garden stepping-stones. Weekdays, he works on aircraft hydraulics and fuel systems in a repair depot at the Cherry Point Marine Corps Air Station, where Kathleen also works. He describes his job as one "with no imagination, no deviation, no anything." Now, as he scoops mighty hollows in the clay and gets ready to pour in the slurry, he smiles with absolute contentment. "You know, the relaxing thing about doing art is, Nothing is wrong."

Everywhere in Becky and Dennis's garden Art with a capital *A* hugs the earth, chaperones the vegetables and flowers, lurks under shrubbery, rears up on its hind legs, or fixes the observer with an all-seeing stare. The garden itself is immense, situated partly in the front yard, partly in the back, and bigger by far than anything the Chief has ever planted at our place. The two-acre lot is nothing but garden and woods, with only a token patch of grass in front of the large, two-story house that they built themselves starting in 1980. In it they've reared two daughters and two sons, the latter of whom still live at home. The dense and shady woods behind the house shelter a pen containing mallards and a wading pool and also the chicken coop lorded over by Leonard, a Rhode Island Red rooster who knows better than to crow all night. "Actually, he's a wimp," Becky says, catching him. His spurred feet kick ineffectually. "I think he's too old for the hens." The coop houses dozens of hens—the "girls," as Becky calls them; one section holds juvenile hens without combs, and another, the grown laying hens that sport fleshy red crests atop their heads. A third section contains four cocky young roosters, one of which will succeed Leonard. I'll go home with a dozen big rosy-brown eggs.

Three strides away from the chicken coop stands the springhouse, Becky's favorite retreat. Unlike Dennis, who was born in Ohio, Becky has lived in coastal Carolina almost all her life; when she was little more than a toddler, her father left the Marine Corps and settled in the town with the post office that serves the Point. She's a tiny, lithe woman in her late forties who weighs in under the 110-pound lower limit for giving blood, but till recently she worked as a mechanic servicing jet engines for Harriers and various helicopters at the same Cherry Point aircraft repair depot in which Dennis spends his unimaginative, undeviating hours. Now she serves as a quality inspector and also as an interpreter, using sign language to facilitate communication between the hearing and the deaf. Her own hearing is acute. Working at the base, though, means dealing all too frequently with locked-in bureaucratic minds and dicta issued by computers. But in the springhouse she finds plants, amphibians, and solace.

No spring wells up in the springhouse, a four-square building with a cathedral ceiling and wraparound windows that flood the place night and day with the light of sun or stars. Below the windows stand long white counters, one with a capacious sink. Here wine bottles are rinsed out and lined up below the windows; their green glass stays filled with nothing but air and light as long as they remain in the springhouse. Neighbors tote empty bottles over here rather than putting them in the recycling bins provided by the county; the reward is often a liter of the current homemade vintage. Coastal Forest Wines, that's what they call this oenological enterprise in which any and all fruit is up for fermenting—from traditional grapes, along with plums grown by Becky's father, Mo, to more exotic stuff like cranberries and bananas. The different vintages are named for family members or, like Millennium Plum Wine, for a significant event. The bottles in the springhouse will be taken as needed to the main house for filling.

Though the springhouse shelters no spring, there's more water at hand than just the well water available through the spigot at the sink. Becky has made a water garden in two fifty-gallon aquaria stationed just inside the entrance. Lush plants rise out of these pools like water nymphs curiously observing life in the world of air. Pickerelweed, gathered in an always brimming drainage ditch just across the road from a correctional unit in the next county, pokes out wide, glossy leaves. In irreverent moments she calls it "prisonweed." The other plants were contributed by friends. Thrusting upward, umbrella plant's spindly stems look like streamside bulrushes. Water poppy's tiny flowers gleam yellow just above the water, and frog bit, resembling miniature lily pads, covers part of the surface. A water hyacinth, close cousin to pickerelweed, shows off a dense cluster of lavender-blue blossoms. *Lavender's blue, dilly, dilly, lavender's green, when I am king, dilly, dilly, you shall be queen*—I am suddenly reminded of the nursery rhyme. But in the wilds water hyacinth is not a lilting or gentle plant; an invader from the Tropics, it's taken over ditches, canals, ponds, lakes throughout the Southeast and made passage through them impossible. Contained in Becky's garden, however, it is not a scourge but rather a plant of considerable, beckoning charm. And amid this bursting vegetation dwells a tutelary spirit, a bullfrog.

Another bullfrog lives outside and, along with some leopard frogs, claims as his territory an outdoor water garden, once a child's wading pool, that rests at the foot of a towering stand of bamboo. Goldfish swim there, too, and toads use it for laying egg strings that hatch into a wriggle of tadpoles. Dennis says, "This pool—did Becky tell you about the moccasin?" No; so I inquire. It turns out that once upon a time, not long ago, when Becky was out in the back section of the garden, she spotted a cottonmouth moccasin in the water. Not about to let it eat her frogs and fish, she got a grabbing stick— a long-shafted pole with a clamp at the nether end—and captured the snake. Holding it at arm's length, she summoned Dennis, who did it in. It's like Becky to look upon a hideously venomous snake and put the well-being of small, tender creatures before her own.

Near the pool grows a plenitude of herbs, vegetables, and flowers in slightly raised beds. Another nursery rhyme surfaces: *Mary, Mary, quite contrary, how does your garden grow; With silver bells and cockleshells and pretty maids all in a row.* Nothing here is in much of a row, but the garden specializes in delightfully incongruous juxtapositions. Herbs growing higgledy-piggledy amid the vegetables scent the air. They include, of course, the well-sung foursome of parsley, sage, rosemary, and thyme (the rosemary was rooted from my great bush). Basil, dill, lovage, and celeriac mingle with Roman chamomile—"It smells so good"—for making a hair rinse, and German chamomile for brewing tea. This year Becky has set in caraway and sesame seeds for the first time and made an initial planting of St.-John's-wort, a notable stress reliever, a panacea that can create calm in the face of any worry-making circumstance, from anticipation of Y2K to finding a predatory moccasin getting set to dine on frogs and goldfish.

And every other inch of space in the back garden is alive with greenery and fruit. Cucumber vines sprawl on the ground over here, and cantaloupe vines over there; between them horseradish raises the white-veined banners of its leaves and birdhouse gourds climb merrily along a chest-high fence; when they're dry, Becky will turn them into feeders, with painted or wood-burned designs, that can hold seeds for titmice and chickadees. Tomatoes, some of them heirloom varieties like 'Brandywine', rise heavy with fruit—big plants, but they're only knee high to a stand of giant sunflowers. Bell peppers and jalapeños rub shoulders with an Italian variety of eggplant trade-named 'Violetta Lunga,' "long purple." Amid the vegetables, flowers lift their colors like gaudy gypsies—here lavender cosmos and orange marigolds, there blue cornflowers, bright yellow coreopsis, and yarrow with reddish umbels. (Yarrow is an anciently honored plant; its long-preserved blossoms and lacy-leaved stalks have been found with some of the young women in Denmark's Neolithic bog graves.) And a Chinese lantern vine, climbing a trellis set against the springhouse wall, casts the light of its red-and-yellow flowers among palmately compound green leaves, five to a cluster and slender as knives. The back garden is almost as inclusive as any garden can be. But there's more elsewhere: chard and wildflowers growing decoratively along the foundation of the house and another full garden in the front yard, where three kinds of pole beans, summer squashes, red potatoes, asparagus, and okra are raised.

Yet there's more you can't see from the road. Mushrooms—not just any old mushrooms but shiitakes—are farmed in a fenced-in enclosure next to the woods on the east side of the yard. In early 1997 Becky and Dennis invested their income tax refund in shiitake plugs. They gathered stout oak and sweet gum logs, drilled them with holes three inches apart, inserted the plugs, and put on a sealant of bee's wax. One on another, the logs are stacked at an angle against a sturdy rail. In the very first year all the money spent on plugs was recouped, with some to spare. In 1999, 120 pounds of shiitakes were harvested on a single January day. Before being marketed, the mushrooms are dried in large, airy fabric tents that hang from the springhouse rafters. But on the day that I come to watch Dennis make a bird, no shiitakes sprout from their parent logs; the weather has been far too dry. Come a break in the summer heat, though, come drizzle and downpour, they'll fruit again.

And still more: Beside the drive a two- by six-foot curvilinear patch holds what Dennis calls Becky's weed relocation project: ragweed, goldenrod, moonflower, dog fennel, bracken ferns, orange daylilies, and bay laurel. All but the sweet-scented moonflower, which was a gift, were dug from local roadsides and transported here. The project is not so addlepated as it sounds; Becky craves acquaintance with the vegetation, ridiculous or sublime, that characterizes the coast. And at the entrance to the front yard she has also set in other plants taken from the wild—prickly pear cactus and the needle-leaved yuccas known as Spanish daggers. Both have burgeoned. Yearly, the yuccas thrust up stalks bearing white, bell-shaped flowers; the prickly pears burst into soft golden blooms that crown the topmost curve of the fleshy, spine-studded leaves.

The two acres regularly produce cornucopious harvests. Becky and Dennis both pick and process the vegetables that their acres yield year after year—and fling themselves into the grinding, can't-stop-till-you're-done labor of canning and preserving food with an energy that tuckers me out just thinking about it. Take the patch of red potatoes in the front-yard garden: It produced enough plump tubers in the summer before Y2K to fill 104 quart jars, plus give a summer's worth of good eating and also a batch of seed potatoes for the next year. More than a hundred quarts! But in his imaginative, deviant hours, Dennis invented a machine to make the peeling of potatoes something that Beetle Bailey, eternally on KP, would envy. The size of a fifty-five-gallon drum, it's made of hardware cloth and powered by an old washing machine motor: Potatoes put in at one end and vigorously tumbled emerge at the other end as naked as newborn babies. With the magical machine, more than two hundred pounds can be peeled in the short space of an hour. Of the stockpile of potatoes and other food—dozens on dozens of jars of tomatoes, beans, jam, and millennial sauerkraut—Dennis says, "I always go overboard. My middle name is Overdo-It."

Every year they overdo it. In 1999, however, there was a special reason: Y2K. They prepared mightily against the possibility that electricity might fail and supermarkets close if computers balked at dealing with the calendar's change from '99 to '00 and thus created serious glitches in supplies of energy, food, banking services, and the other necessities of increasingly urbanized society. In the energy department they've always been independent, heating with wood, a renewable source of fuel. Then, like most of us at the Point, Dennis and Becky have hooked up to the county's water system but use the existing well for things like watering the gardens and making birds of bioglop. Their well is fitted with an electric pump, but Dennis contrived a fail-safe manually operated pump to pull up water from the subterranean depths.

But they were hardly panicked by the potential for computerized snafus that could put kinks and crinkles into the fabric of the world. Rather, the two of them, touching earth, have long been in the habit of making preparations for any eventuality. It's a way of saying, "Yes! We can do it all by ourselves!" And I am sure that no matter what will come to be, fair weather or foul, they'll still be doing it themselves twenty years from now.

And everywhere, everywhere—amid the vegetables and flowers, beside the chicken coop and the relocated weeds, at the entrance, along the frontage on the road, there's deviation, there's Art with a capital *A*. It's part and parcel of the thrust toward self-sufficiency: evidence of an ability to bring into being things—ornaments, pleasures, little simulacra of the garden gods—that are as necessary to the spirit as food and breath are to the body. Some are modest: small, stout mushrooms made of bioconcrete rise in the weed relocation project, and a turtle the size of a pie plate spraddles at its edge. Rings with carved designs circle around some plants to serve as edging; bowls of many shapes and sizes act as flowerpots. Some are startling: A trio of gleaming white heads, as self-possessed as those on Easter Island but fashioned in miniature, sit on tree stumps and guard the entrance to the front yard. The largest is King; his mate, Queen, observes the world from just behind him on his left. *(When I am king, dilly, dilly, you shall be queen.)* And behind him to the right sits Prince. Their features are sharp, their expressions proprietary, their smiles all-knowing. Southernwood, an *Artemisia* that bears little purple flowers on slender stems, springs from King's head; Queen was molded wearing a garden hat with a frilly brim. Another head, not bioconcrete but carved of wood, rests beside the front walk; it looks downright piratical—black captain's hat atop long, wind-tousled hair, eyes squinched against the sun, full red lips pursed in a full-gun sneer. Still another head, made of blond wood and possessed of a friendly, toothy grin, is stationed beside the front door to the house; its hat is a pot of trailing ferns. Nor are these the end of the garden's wooden presences. Like the original, this Eden is not without its serpents. Sinuous branches downed in storms have been transformed into snakes: One has inset golden eyes and wood-burned scales; the other, made of an sixteen-foot oak limb, writhes toward the house like a full-sized python. Becky's father, Mo, a skilled woodcarver, has added recently to the menagerie by fashioning an owl, a toad, and a turtle in running shoes out of blocks of storm-downed wood.

And over here, near the road in a future garden only recently cleared of trees, the rusty skeleton of a dinosaur rears up on its powerful hind legs. Its mouth gapes wide; at any moment it may announce its presence with a brooling Jurassic roar. Its origin, however, is not swamp but scrap heap. This *Tyrannosaurus* is a junk sculpture welded by Dennis, with ribs made of barrel hoops, legs and backbone of pipe, and the massive head and great nail-studded jaws of machined metal. Dennis originally used a motorcycle gas tank for the head, but it proved too fragile to withstand the weather, so he rooted through his scraps of metal for material to make a more substantial cranium. I take a photo of Becky and Dennis's elder son approaching it head-on, as if to fight; at six feet, it's taller than he. But it turns out to have a benign side after all: A Carolina wren has built a nest behind the sharp teeth.

And now there's a bird under way. Back at the pile of sandy clay the kittens are still playing, though Snarf is gone (later we'll find him in the house). Sweating merrily, Dennis is digging out more molds, this time for planters. And Becky's digging, making a squared-off depression for another planter; a rectangular bin will be placed upside down in the cavity, and the bioconcrete will be poured between the clay and the bin. Suddenly, I cannot resist getting my own hands dirty. We are kids in a sand pile. Scoop out a hollow the shape of a small bowl, add two narrow troughs at each side and a larger one at the bowl's north end—domed shell, legs, and head: Box turtle. Or I hope it will be a turtle; what will emerge from this mold and all the others made today depends on skill—or lack of it—and on the weather. Heat and sun will advance the curing of the bioconcrete; rain will slow it down. Then Dennis says, "You want a birdbath?" Of course! In one corner of the clay heap he excavates a mold for the pedestal with a posthole digger; just below that he scrapes away clay and shapes a large circle with a raised center for the bowl. A few finishing touches on the molds, and that's it—time to pour in the gloppy mixture of peat moss, cement, and sand. Ordinarily this mixture dries white, but today some of it has been colored red or black with cement dye that Becky found at Lowe's and saved for an occasion such as this. Dennis first transfers the stuff from the mixer to a red wheelbarrow, then shovels it from the wheelbarrow into the molds. He's covered with slurry up to his elbows; his face wears freckles of bioconcrete. When he's done, Becky asks if she should get plastic bags to cover the day's creations so that they don't dry out too fast. "Nope," Dennis says. "Earth'll take care of them." And we all use the hose upon ourselves to wash off clay and bioconcrete.

Two days later I'm summoned for the grand disinterment. Dennis washes clay off the latest Art with hose at full throttle. Out come the new creations, one by one. The rectangular planter has suffered a split, but that can be mended, can be glued together with a little more slurry. The birdbath, with its red pedestal and bowl, has survived, and so has my turtle, cast in black. According to Dennis's instructions, I'll finish it off later, refining it with a screwdriver and a chip of cinder block. As for the bird that inaugurated this round of deviation, we aren't at all certain about what species it might be. Its posture is upright, like that of a hawk perched on a branch; the black wings lie close to the body; the great rust-red head is hunched between the shoulders. It is massive, brooding, prehistoric. We decide at first that it must be a Dennisodactyl. But that evening I find its picture in the National Geographic *Field Guide to the Birds of North America: Gymnogyps californianus*, "naked vulture native to California." It's a California condor. And all the way across the continent, here at Great Neck Point, just behind the patch that held potatoes earlier and is now home to a mess of pole beans in Becky and Dennis's front yard, it perches, standing sentinel, on a tree stump. I doubt that anything—drought, hurricane, or fleeting time —will soon do it in. It is a meet emblem for the sprawling, quirky zest for life found in this house, these gardens.

Millennial Sauerkraut

IN COASTAL North Carolina cabbage plants may be set out in the garden in mid-February. Slowly, slowly, the outer leaves burgeon from tender ovals not much bigger than the palm of a child's hand into huge, upright, green things almost as big as an elephant's ear. Within their protective toughness, the magic happens, the sweet heads form, some globe shaped, others pointed, depending on the variety set out. The few cabbages that the Chief plants for our own use tend to be considerate; a dozen plants do not usually mature simultaneously but rather present themselves piecemeal, one today, the next in three or four days' time, two more a week later. Fresh cabbage saves well, but it's not amenable to canning or freezing, for heat and cold break down the fibers. The answer to preservation is sauerkraut.

People in the Middle Ages ate sauerkraut. An old saying has it that "He who sows cabbages and fattens a pig will get through the winter." And kraut is good for you, for it preserves the vitamin C in cabbage. Captain James Cook doled out daily rations of sauerkraut to his crews and credited it with saving them from scurvy.

Our garden, alas, never yields enough curvular pearls for making kraut. During my first decade at the Point, however, commercial gardens produced enough cabbages to fill half a dozen tractor-trailers and then some. When the trailers were full, excess cabbages and culls were put at the roadside for any passerby to pick up and use. But the bottom dropped out of the cabbage market in the mid-1990s, and it was no longer economical to plant and tend acres of tightly packed green globes. What were lovers of sauerkraut to do?

Becky and Dennis solved the problem in their drive to put up enough viands to beat any mischief that might be caused by the arrival of Y2K. In the summer of 1999 they bought a thousand pounds—half a ton!—of cabbages for a nickel a pound from a farm downriver, gave away more than half of it, and put up a good four hundred pounds. Overdo it? Not really, for much of the kraut was given away; the Chief and I received forty pounds. Mmm, Reuben sandwiches, relish for hot dogs, and some just for eating plain.

Becky's recipe is far easier than the usual instructions that call not only for a crock of cabbage covered by a weighted board or plate but also for the regular skimming off of scum as the cabbage ferments. The bags that she and Dennis use to hold the fermenting cabbage are clear, not black or green—a clever idea, for this way you can see both process and product. Incidentally, iodized salt may be used, but beware: It will turn the kraut pink.

NECESSARY SUPPLIES
1 clean 33-gallon trash can or a wastebasket
   big enough to hold the cabbage to be processed
3 33-gallon plastic trash bags

INGREDIENTS
cabbages, shredded or coarsely chopped, in 5-pound batches
uniodized salt, 2½ tablespoons for each 5 pounds of cabbage

PUT THE SHREDDED CABBAGE, 5 pounds at a time, into one of the 33-gallon trash bags. Add 2½ tablespoons uniodized salt. Shake the mixture, and shake it, and shake it some more.

PUT THE BAG with cabbage and salt into the clean trash can. Press the cabbage down with your fingers.

SHRED another 5 pounds. Add it along with 2½ more tablespoons of salt to the cabbage already in the bag in the trash can. Stir and shake. Keep packing and salting the shredded cabbage, 5 pounds at a time, until you have enough.

PUT THE 2 REMAINING trash bags one inside the other to make a double thickness. (Two bags are used to eliminate the possibility of leaks.) Place the doubled trash bags on top of the cabbage—not on top of the bag containing the cabbage but within that bag, on top of the cabbage itself. Put 2 or 3 inches of water into the doubled bags. Use your fingers to press the bags against the cabbage and the wall of the container. The bags will then sit firmly atop the cabbage and make a seal.

PLACE THE CONTAINER with cabbage in a cool, dark place like a cellar. An ideal temperature is 60 degrees; it may be higher, however. In any event, try to make sure that the temperature holds steady.

CHECK THE CABBAGE as it ferments. After 3 or 4 weeks at 60 degrees or only 2 weeks at 70 degrees—when the kraut is properly soured—it can be stored in glass jars in the refrigerator. Or to save fridge space, it can be canned.

TO CAN SAUERKRAUT, heat it to a simmer and place it in hot canning jars. A teaspoon of salt may be added to each pint of kraut. Process in a water bath for 30 minutes. Remove the jars and wait for them to make that rewarding *ping* as they seal.

SERVES BATTALIONS

Joyce's Great Neck Vegetable Casserole

BECKY SERVES a splendidly all-inclusive vegetable casserole. The recipe came from her mother, Joyce, a fine down-home cook, who called it her "funeral casserole" and said, "There's a funeral and people to feed. I'm stuck out here in the country twenty-three miles from town. Everybody carries cakes and pies, but who wants all that sweet? I take vegetables. You start by looking in the fridge—or in the garden, if the season's right."

No need to wait for a funeral (though I hope someone carried this casserole to Joyce's own wake in 1994). The dish will do nicely for a potluck supper or a celebration—or simply, as Becky says, to clean out the refrigerator. The ingredients set out below are far from canonical. Start, of course, by opening the fridge and seeing what's inside. Then add to the dish as you see fit. The only essentials are onions, tomatoes, sugar, salt, butter, and tapioca.

INGREDIENTS

1½ cups sliced onions

2 cups celery, cut into 2-inch pieces

1½ cups carrots, peeled, cut into strips,
  and parboiled for 3 minutes

2 cups green beans, frozen or fresh, snapped or French cut

½ cup green bell pepper, cut into strips or small chunks

2 cups tomatoes, canned or fresh with skins removed

2½ teaspoons salt (less may be used)

2 tablespoons sugar

¼ cup tapioca

¼ cup butter

PREHEAT the oven to 350 degrees.

ADD OTHER VEGETABLES if you wish: butterbeans, peas, broccoli, cut corn, small chunks of cabbage, summer squash sliced into rounds, a tad of okra, a diced turnip, and whatever else your garden (or refrigerator) yields. But beware of any vegetable with a flavor so strong that it would overwhelm its milder neighbors; rutabaga is a potent example.

MIX THE VEGETABLES together, then layer them in a baking dish. Sprinkle salt, sugar, and tapioca over each layer. Dot each layer generously with butter.

BAKE, COVERED, for 1½ to 2½ hours. (Fresh vegetables take longer than the canned or precooked kind.) Uncover for the last 30 minutes of cooking.

SERVES a starving horde or a modest few, depending on the size of the casserole

FEASTS

AS MUCH AS WE ADMIRE the vegetables—their earth-inspired colors, their shapes that range from plump to gawky, their textures that are smooth to lightly furred, their venerable histories—we grow them to be eaten. An ordinary meal that includes homegrown produce becomes extraordinary. It's special and certainly better than anything prepared strictly from supermarket stuff, which all too often bears signs of age—wrinkles, flabbiness, soft touches of decay. Eating what we grow always brings a feeling of celebration. Seeds and sweat, tender shoots and dirty hands have been transformed by gardening magic into food for body and soul.

And here's a round dozen of our favorite recipes.

Confetti Beans in Casserole

ONCE UPON A TIME it was considered most polite to cook beans whole. In her 1824 cookbook Mary Randolph issues explicit directions for cooking "French beans." Referring to the slender haricot sort, much relished in France, she says: "To send up the beans whole, when they

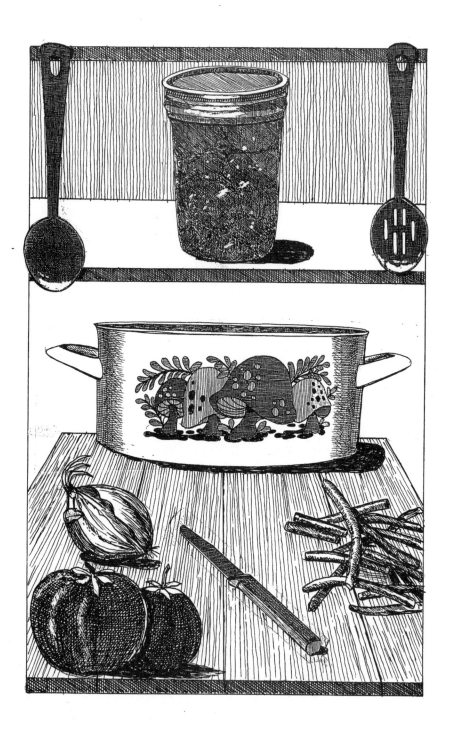

are young, is much the best method, and their delicate flavour and colour is much better preserved. When a little more grown, they must be cut lengthwise in thin slices after stringing; and for common tables, they are split, and divided across; but those who are nice, do not use them at such a growth as to require splitting."

For this recipe, any kind of green bean will do—haricot, wax, 'Blue Lake', 'Kentucky Wonder', other varieties, most of them developed these days so that there's no need to pull off any strings. But heed the advice of Mary Randolph just the same: the younger, the better. If you wish, however, to "cut them across"—snap them, that is—go right ahead; or cook them whole, as you prefer. Use as many beans as you wish, and add the other ingredients proportionately. I usually make the dish in accord with how many beans fit into a casserole appropriate to the occasion—a one-quart baking dish for the Chief and me, something considerably larger if there's company. To judge amounts, the rule of thumb has it that a pound of beans, weighed before stemming, makes approximately six servings. The recipe may be frozen but loses quality from the first moment. It's better by far to put leftovers, if any, into the refrigerator and polish them off at the next possible occasion.

INGREDIENTS
1 pound freshly picked green or wax beans, stemmed
4 medium onions, diced
1 red bell pepper, diced
salt
paprika
butter

PREHEAT the oven to 350 degrees.

LIGHTLY GREASE a baking dish. Place layers of vegetables in it, beginning and ending with beans.

SPRINKLE SALT and paprika lightly on each layer. Dot each layer with thin-sliced pats of butter.

BAKE, covered, for 1¼ hours, or till the beans are tender.

Lima Beans with Onions and Tomatoes

ONCE UPON A TIME, a version of this scrumptious combination was available in the frozen-food section of the grocery store. But for some peculiar reason having to do, perhaps, with marketing, it dropped out of sight several decades ago and has not reappeared since. The rule of thumb here is that a pound of lima beans in the pod suffices for two servings. The dish freezes well enough so that September's limas can be served up at Thanksgiving.

INGREDIENTS
1 pound freshly picked limas in the pod
2 tablespoons butter
1 medium onion, diced
1 clove garlic, mashed
1 small tomato, peeled, seeded, and chopped fine
salt to taste

SHELL THE LIMAS and put them into a saucepan. Add barely enough water to cover. Put a lid on the saucepan and simmer for about 15 minutes.

AS THE LIMAS are simmering, melt the butter in a skillet and sauté the onion till it's transparent, about 5 minutes.

POUR THE WATER off the limas. Add the garlic, tomato, and onion (and a tad more butter, if you wish). Stirring occasionally, simmer for 5 to 10 minutes. Add salt to taste and serve.

Dried Beans #1: Leather Britches Beans

MO, OUR NEIGHBOR, father of my compatriot Becky, and one of the Point's more experienced gardeners, uses this old-timey method of preserving beans, an example of country thrift, which he learned while growing up on farms in Illinois and Indiana.

NECESSARY SUPPLIES
needle
heavy-duty thread

INGREDIENTS
as many edible (but not overripe) green or yellow beans
as you wish to dry

PUT THE THREADED needle through the tip of each bean and keep stringing the beans along the thread until you have at least enough for a meal. Hang the beans in a dry place. They will indeed dry out to a leathery consistency.

TO PREPARE them for eating, take as many as you need for a meal. Soak them in a saucepan for 1 or 2 hours to render the leather edible. Drain off all but enough water to cover the beans.

BRING THE SAUCEPAN to a boil; then reduce the heat and cook the beans till they are tender, about 20 minutes, possibly more. Keep sampling. They will be chewier than fresh-picked beans, but oh, the flavor when they're seasoned with dollops of butter.

Dried Beans #2: Chief's Mess Navy Bean Soup

IT'S NOT MUCH harder to dry beans for soup than it is to buy them at the supermarket. When the pods of green and wax beans, limas, or speckled butterbeans grow bursting fat and turn brown, with seeds rattling inside, they can be picked individually and further dried. One good variety for drying is 'Kentucky Wonder', a pole type of string bean with brown seeds. You can also grow shelling varieties, like navy, pinto, and black beans. One handy-dandy way of drying the full pods is to put to work the summertime heat in the interior of a closed-up car. Spread the pods on cardboard trays, and place the trays on the backseat. In no more than a week the beans will be ready to shell and store. Another method, used for preserving large quantities of dried beans, is to pull up whole plants when the bean pods begin to dry and then hang them indoors to dry for a week or two. When the pods are dry as a desert, the beans may be shelled out by hand or threshed by banging them inside a clean trash can or bucket. Let the wind blow away the chaff by pouring the dried beans slowly onto a heavy cloth outdoors on a briskly breezy day; repeat the pouring for as long as it takes to get rid of the bits of pod, stems, and leaves.

Navy beans are the white seeds of one of the many incarnations of *Phaseolus vulgaris.* And navy bean soup is a favorite of the Chief, who spent more than twenty years aboard ships and naval bases. I came to make it this way:

"I miss navy bean soup," he said. Not much later he made his desires more explicit. "I want navy bean soup. I *crave* navy bean soup. I'd do anything—well, almost—to get some."

The only possible response to such importuning was to make navy bean soup. I bought a package of dried beans, stirred them up, and presented it to him proudly at supper one evening.

"What's this?" he said.

"What you've been asking for—navy bean soup."

"No, it's not. In fact, it's all wrong."

I was much taken aback. "How so? It's made with the right beans."

"Navy bean soup is white, but you've put tomatoes in this stuff." He ate it anyhow, nor did he have difficulty spooning it down right smartly. It just wasn't navy bean soup.

So I proceeded to experiment and finally came up with a concoction that passes muster. We serve it with grilled cheese sandwiches—Swiss or Gouda—and applesauce, that sine qua non, which adds a touch of sweetness as well as acting as a supposedly fail-safe antidote to the infamous Problem.

Contrary to instructions given on many packages of dried beans, navy beans need not be presoaked before cooking but can simply be placed as is into the stockpot. They'll soften nicely.

The recipe is amenable to freezing with minimum loss of quality.

INGREDIENTS

2 cups dried navy beans

2 quarts water

¼ pound lean salt pork, diced

1 beef bouillon cube

3 cloves garlic, minced, or ¼ teaspoon garlic powder

¼ teaspoon dried marjoram

⅛ teaspoon freshly ground black pepper

1 large onion, diced

1 rib celery, diced

1 medium potato, peeled and cut into small cubes

salt to taste

PLACE THE NAVY BEANS, water, salt pork, bouillon cube, garlic, marjoram, and pepper in a stockpot. Bring to a boil, then reduce the heat
and simmer for 2 hours.

ADD THE ONION, celery, and potato. Simmer for 1 more hour. Add salt
to taste and serve.

SERVES 6 HANDILY

Frozen Sliced Sweet Dill Pickles

CUCUMBERS—eat them fresh or make pickles. Pickling is the only way
to preserve them as anything more than insubstantial memories of
summer. Luckily, generations of good cooks have handed down
their recipes: sweet relishes, piccalilly, eight-day pickle chips, and
this one—frozen cucumber pickles. It comes to me from my Aunt
Caye, now on the near edge of ninety and in a nursing home.
Where she got the recipe, I do not know. I can guarantee, however,
that it's delicious. And not just that but also easy to make. It's not
necessary to use the small pickling cucumbers called for in the
recipe if all you have is a large variety. Simply slice them thin, as
directed. But do not remove the peel, for that's the only location of
vitamin A.

INGREDIENTS
1 pound 3-inch cucumbers, sliced ⅛ inch thick
   (about 4 cups packed)
¾ pound yellow onions, sliced ⅛ inch thick (about 2 cups)
4 teaspoons uniodized salt
2 tablespoons water
¾–1 cup sugar

½ cup cider vinegar

1 teaspoon dried dill weed

(or 1 tablespoon fresh, if you have it)

MIX the cucumbers, onions, salt, and water in a 2-quart bowl that is not aluminum. Let stand for 2 hours. Drain but do not rinse. Return the vegetables to the bowl.

ADD the sugar, vinegar, and dill. Let stand, stirring occasionally, until the sugar has dissolved completely and liquid covers the vegetables.

PACK in containers. Seal tightly and freeze.

TO SERVE, defrost in the refrigerator or at room temperature. Return what's not used to the fridge, where it can handily be stored till it's all gone.

Tomato and Eggplant Sauce

EGGPLANT—some years we grow the round, fat kind, and some years we add a slender, elongated Japanese variety. I love the leisurely sound of the European word for the plant—*aubergine,* a word originally Sanskrit but transformed over the millennia by its passage through Arabic, Catalan, and French. I rejoice in the glossy midnight purple of the eggplant's skin and relish the slightly peppery flavor of its ample flesh. At our house it often ends up dipped in egg, rolled in seasoned crumbs, and sautéed in butter till it's crispy. (Eggplant excels indeed at soaking up butter, but see below for a way to keep it from being a sponge.) Or it may be sliced, put into an ovenproof dish, and baked with layers of tomatoes, onions, and Parmesan cheese. Ah, Parmigiana!

The flesh of eggplant is abundantly blessed with intercellular air pockets. When it's sautéed, those pockets sop up butter or cooking oil. The secret of keeping eggplant fat-free is to slice it into rounds, salt the slices, and leave them out for an hour. Before cooking, rinse off the salt and pat the slices dry. Then fry them till they're crisp.

Eggplant cannot be canned at all; nor does it take kindly to freezing, except—thank goodness for exceptions—when it's cooked in a casserole with other vegetables. Alas, there's never enough Parmigiana left over to put in the freezer. Eggplant is, of course, available in any supermarket during the winter, but it's not the same—not so fresh—as one grown in the garden, nor has it ever been an intimate part of our summer days. How to save our own roly-poly produce? To my rescue came a recipe from the cooking section that appears every Wednesday in the local paper. The recipe specifically instructs that it be used as a sauce for pasta, but it's equally good over rice or, even better, as a side dish on its own. Over the last ten years I've changed the recipe a bit, mainly by increasing the proportions of some ingredients, especially eggplant and garlic. And for all those years it has granted my wish for the warm summer taste of homegrown eggplant, tomatoes, and herbs in the cold white deeps of winter.

INGREDIENTS

1 large onion, diced

1 medium bell pepper, diced

6 cloves garlic, sliced thin

2 teaspoons dried basil leaves,
    or 4 teaspoons finely chopped fresh basil leaves

1 teaspoon dried oregano,
    or 2 teaspoons finely chopped fresh oregano

2 tablespoons olive oil

4 cups tomatoes, peeled and cut into chunks

2 cups eggplant, peeled and cut into 1-inch cubes

salt and pepper

SAUTÉ the onion, bell pepper, garlic, basil, and oregano in olive oil till the onion is translucent, about 5 minutes.

STIR in the tomatoes and eggplant. Cook, covered, over medium-high heat for 5 minutes.

UNCOVER and cook over medium heat till the eggplant is tender and the mixture has thickened to your liking, about 15 to 20 minutes. Season with salt and pepper to taste.

MAKES approximately 3 pints; freezes well in plastic freezer bags or boxes

Eggplant Parmigiana

IT WOULDN'T be fair to mention Parmigiana without providing our recipe. It's a variation on one given in *Too Many Tomatoes, Squash, Beans, and Other Good Things,* the cookbook on what to do with full-to-bursting gardens. The recipe also helps use up and preserve overabundant tomatoes. The wine sauce is most amenable to freezing and can be added to dishes like beef stew and vegetable soup as well as to Parmigiana.

INGREDIENTS

2 medium eggplants, unpeeled

¼ cup flour

olive oil

3 cloves garlic, minced

6 medium tomatoes, peeled and chopped

1 onion, chopped fine

1 rib celery, chopped fine

1 tablespoon minced fresh parsley,
    or 1½ teaspoons dried parsley

1 tablespoon finely chopped fresh basil,
    or 1½ teaspoons dried basil

¼ teaspoon salt

¼ teaspoon sugar

¼ teaspoon pepper

½ cup red wine

½ cup grated Parmesan cheese

1 pound various cheeses,
    such as Fontina and mozzarella, sliced thin

PREHEAT the oven to 350 degrees.

SLICE the eggplants ½ inch thick, dip them in flour, and fry them in oil over high heat until soft. Set aside.

IN A SAUCEPAN, mix together the garlic, tomatoes, onion, celery, parsley, basil, salt, sugar, and pepper with 2 tablespoons of olive oil. Simmer vigorously for 30 minutes.

ADD the wine to the mixture. Continue simmering until the sauce thickens, 15 to 20 minutes.

IN A GREASED baking dish, layer the eggplant and sauce. Top with cheeses.

BAKE for 30 to 40 minutes.

SERVES 6

Eggplant Minestrone

HERE'S ANOTHER recipe adapted from *Too Many Tomatoes,* which unaccountably does not include beans in its list of ingredients. In my book minestrone *must* have beans. The ones I've used most recently were dried beans produced by both our 'Blue Lake' and brittle wax bush varieties. This recipe also freezes well.

INGREDIENTS

1 large onion, chopped

2 cloves garlic, minced

2 tablespoons olive oil

1 medium eggplant, peeled and diced

3 carrots, diced

2 ribs celery, diced

8 large tomatoes, peeled and quartered

4 cups beef stock

1 teaspoon dried oregano

1 teaspoon dried basil

1 teaspoon salt

1 teaspoon sugar

½ cup orrecchio (small shells)

¼ teaspoon pepper

1 14.5-ounce can kidney beans, drained and rinsed

IN A LARGE STOCKPOT, sauté the onion and garlic in the oil for 5 minutes.

ADD the eggplant and cook for 3 minutes.

ADD the carrots, celery, tomatoes, beef stock, oregano, basil, salt, and sugar to the stockpot. Simmer, uncovered, for 1 to 2 hours.

ADD the orrecchio and pepper. Simmer for 20 minutes.

ADD the beans and simmer for 2 to 3 minutes, until the beans are heated through.

SERVES 8

Potatoes Baked with Herbs

A SAVORY potpourri of herb garden scents and flavors—that's what this recipe calls for. And you can cater to your own tastes—be as freewheeling as you wish in selecting herbs to complement the potatoes. My favorite combination is parsley, chives, sage, and lemon thyme, picked fresh, mixed together, and chopped fine. But other herbs work equally well, like oregano, savory, and rosemary. The chopping helps release the vital oils. The recipe as given below serves four; for fewer or more people, adjust the ingredients accordingly.

INGREDIENTS
4 medium well-shaped potatoes
1 teaspoon salt
2–3 tablespoons butter, melted
2–3 tablespoons fresh herbs,
    or 2–3 teaspoons of the dried variety
¼ cup grated cheddar cheese
1½ tablespoons grated Parmesan cheese

PREHEAT the oven to 425 degrees.

PEEL the potatoes if their skin is tough. Otherwise just scrub and rinse them.

CUT the potatoes into ¼-inch slices—but not quite all the way through. Put them into a baking dish, and fan them slightly.

SPRINKLE the potatoes with salt, and drizzle them with butter. Sprinkle with herbs.

BAKE for about 50 minutes. Remove the dish from the oven and top with cheeses. Bake for another 10 to 15 minutes, till the cheeses are melted and slightly browned and the potatoes are soft inside.

NOTE: Leftovers, if any, may be chopped and folded into an omelet.

Butternut Pie

HOW VERSATILE, the winter squashes! They may be halved and baked with a strip of bacon lying lengthwise or with butter and brown sugar in the bowl that used to hold seeds. They can be pureed and served up with salt, pepper, and lots of butter. Or the puree may become the basic ingredient for butternut soup, butternut bread, butternut pie, butternut cheesecake, and butternut cookies. To make a puree, I steam halved butternuts till they're soft. (For foods of a good size, a fish poacher makes a fine steamer; it will hold two large or three medium butternuts at one time.) Then the pulp is scooped out and put through a Foley food mill. I usually process squash for several hours at a time so that there'll be enough for supper and also for a number of plastic pint and pint-and-a-half boxes to be stashed in the freezer. Whenever a recipe calls for pumpkin, butternut may be most satisfactorily employed instead.

Aside from which, home-processed pumpkins tend to have in-edible strings lining their interiors, and a zillion of them must be removed before you get at the meat. (You can grow relatively string-less pumpkins specially bred for pie making. Don't look to buy them, though, at the stands selling Hallowe'en pumpkins.) But butternuts —acorns and Hubbards, for that matter—come with no strings attached.

INGREDIENTS

½ cup brown sugar

3 tablespoons white sugar

¾ teaspoon salt

¾ cup dark corn syrup

4 eggs

1 teaspoon ground cinnamon

½ teaspoon ground ginger

⅛ teaspoon ground cloves

dash nutmeg

2 cups heavy cream

1½ pints butternut puree

1 teaspoon vanilla

2 9-inch piecrusts

PREHEAT the oven to 425 degrees.

BLEND well the brown sugar, white sugar, salt, corn syrup, eggs, cin-namon, ginger, cloves, and nutmeg.

ADD the cream, butternut, and vanilla to the mixture, stirring well. The mixture will be soupy.

PLACE the piecrusts on a cookie sheet and pour in the mixture. Bake for 1 hour, or till a knife inserted into the filling comes out clean.

MAKES 2 9-inch deep-dish pies

Butternut Bread

THIS BREAD is the perfect way to avoid even the thought of giving anyone a fruitcake. It tastes like holidays—dark, sweet, rich, with a hint of gingerbread—and it also freezes well. Packaged in colorful plastic wrap, decked with a bow and a sprig of pine or holly, it serves as a flavorsome present. No need, however, to save it for special occasions. Its presence at lunch or supper turns any meal into a celebration.

INGREDIENTS
3½ cups flour
3 cups sugar
1 cup vegetable oil
4 eggs
1½ pints mashed butternut
1½ teaspoons salt
1 teaspoon ground cinnamon
1 teaspoon ground nutmeg
2 teaspoons baking soda dissolved in ⅔ cup water

PREHEAT the oven to 350 degrees.

LIGHTLY GREASE 3 bread pans.

MIX together all the ingredients, adding the 2 teaspoons of soda dissolved in water before the batter is entirely smooth. Fill each bread pan about two-thirds full.

BAKE for 1 hour.

COOL. Then wrap the loaves in plastic (I save supermarket produce bags for this purpose) and store them in the refrigerator.

MAKES 3 loaves

Grandma's Tomato Soup

TOMATOES—many of the recipes given so far feature them, along with eggplants and limas. But here's a recipe in which they star as the prime ingredient. It came to us from the neighbor two doors downriver who supplied Dorothy with the old recipe for Peruvian sauce. He grows and cans quart on quart of tomatoes every summer— whole fruit, juice, relishes, and this soup, which is his mother's favorite. The original recipe called for oleo, rather than butter—an ingredient that dates it at least back to the 1940s. And I've changed the amount of sugar called for because the two cups prescribed by the original recipe makes the soup as sweet as a lollipop and conceals the great tomato flavor. The ingredients may be doubled or halved, depending on how much soup you wish to make. The soup will be thick. It can be used as is or thinned with milk or water.

INGREDIENTS
2 cups diced celery
2 cups diced onions
2 cups diced carrots
8 quarts homemade tomato juice (but store-bought will do)
1 cup sugar
10 teaspoons salt
1 teaspoon chili powder

1 pound butter

2 cups flour

COOK the celery, onions, and carrots. Blend the cooked vegetables.

HEAT the juice, sugar, salt, and chili powder. To this liquid, add the vegetable mixture.

MELT the butter and add the flour to it, stirring till the mixture is smooth. Add this thickener to the juice. Heat to a boil, then can in hot jars. (There's no need to process in a water bath.)

MAKES 16 pints, plus at least 2 bowls for supper

The recipes could go on—more soups, more casseroles, more bean and eggplant dishes, not to mention cabbage seasoned with dill butter and broccoli baked with cheese and stuffing. We hope you'll enjoy what's given here as much as we do. *Bon appétit!*

TOUCHING EARTH

SEPTEMBER: ANTAIOS'S CHILDREN have taken over; sicklepod, ragweed, and wire grass reign. Dog fennel veils parts of the garden with huge panicles of tiny white flowers; they look like foaming waterfalls. The cypress vines still bloom scarlet on the tomato cages they have co-opted. But amid the weeds the bell peppers and eggplants demonstrate remarkable obstinacy, continuing to flower and set fruit. The peppers, especially, like the cooling temperatures.

October: We put the garden to bed. But that's the wrong way to describe our autumnal behavior. What we do is not so gentle as putting anything to bed. No stories read, no lullabies to send the garden into its winter dormancy. A term that I've heard used is *strike the garden.* That's closer to the rough truth. I yank up the tomato cages, strip off the dried and clinging vines, and stash the cages two deep in a line along New Field's hedgerow. Riding the lawn tractor like a juggernaut, Chief roars up and down both gardens to mow down the weeds. Then, assaulted one last time by the tiller, the earth is laid open, is stripped bare. Only the eggplants and bell peppers are exempt from ravagement, for by some miracle they continue to

[201]

produce, and the third week in October, just before we migrate, they offer sleek fruits to take north. To our wonderment, they are still bearing when we return for several weeks in November to watch as a marine contractor begins the long job of repairing the hurricane-blasted seawall (fair weather or foul, seawalls are ever in need of attention). I pick the small fruits, then bake eggplant rounds and pepper strips with tomatoes, crushed garlic, and Fontina cheese. The plants are done now; the next day, with a twinge of sadness, I pull them up and put them in the Will-Be.

But the harvest is in and safely stowed. Dirt no longer rests beneath our fingernails; the sweat has dried. For the most part we've succeeded once again in bringing to fruition delights for both body and spirit. Yet all the while, as we move contemplatively through the cool blue days of fall, I am aware that people weren't designed for gardening.

Biology ordained us to a hunting-gathering niche. Men ranged near and far looking for meat, be it mammoth, bison, horse, squirrel, seal, or a mess of fish. Women pretty much stayed home collecting local goodies like nuts, berries, tubers, birds' eggs, insects, and seaweed. When the food ran out in one place, people pulled up stakes and tramped to another, sometimes seasonally, sometimes as feast or famine dictated. Anatomy designates us as omnivores with a lot of dietary flexibility. Along with vitamins and minerals, our chemistry requires a balanced mix of carbohydrates that supply glucose to the body, especially the brain; fats that give energy to muscles; and flesh-building proteins. Our jaws and teeth were made powerful for chewing meat; the motion of those jaws was designed to make short work of whatever we put into our mouths. According to biology, it was never our role to put seeds in the ground, tend the plot, and reap a harvest, though it well may be that we decided somewhere along the line that we'd like to be in charge of our own food supply. So being as we are, big-brained and pushy, we figured out how to tame animals and domesticate plants some twelve to fourteen thousand years ago. Life hasn't been the same since.

We've also figured out how to stay put, a condition that some natural philosophers believe has led to a host of pathologies. Small bands of cooperative friends and relatives have been replaced by anonymous metropolitan concatenations. Social ranking has entered the human equation, with a mort of peasants and outright slaves starving at the bottom, a handful of rulers and executives battening at the top, the rest of us higgledy-piggledy in between and making do as best we can. Then, with our ability to stay put, war has raised its clubs and swords, has dropped its bombs; everything is subject to bloody dispute—land, resources, power, and bald me-firstism. And there's the skeletal testimony. The fossil record indicates that learning to stay in one place has worked other kinds of havoc on human well-being. According to a recent book that summarizes studies made by the anthropologist Clark Spencer Larsen of preagricultural and agricultural sites on St. Catherines Island off the Georgia coast, the teeth of the farmers show more decay than those of their hunting-gathering predecessors, their bones attest to a greater incidence of disease, and they were noticeably shorter. The prehistoric people who colonized the New World also had an average height a good five inches shorter than that of the Cro-Magnons in Europe. Only since the industrial revolution have vitamins and medical technology brought the height and weight of people in the developed world back to early levels. (In the United States a certain amount of inanition, combined with fast-foodism, has brought the weight of many

Americans far above the prehistoric optimum.) What pushed us into taking control of our food supply? Larsen says that we were forced to abandon hunting and gathering, a way of life that afforded us health and security, simply because we had run out of room for our burgeoning populations to continue to live as we had. We had backed ourselves into a corner by occupying every last part of the world in which we could support ourselves by nuts and tubers here, fish and mammoths there.

Since we settled down, the earth has been abused, of course. This sad truth was recognized long ago. Pliny introduces his subjects with verve; he is patently glad to champion the earth's cause, to write about her grains, gardens, and flowers. "Consider the variety of plants, their numbers, flowers, fragrances, and colors," he writes, "and also the juices and virtues Earth engenders for human well-being and pleasure." But he follows these remarks with a caveat: Earth also brings us to think of her as the producer of harmful things, but in doing so, "we impute to her our own crimes." In Pliny's view there are brambles among the race of man.

We do commit crimes of greed. We do rob the soil of fertility and denude the land. Genetic engineering may also be a crime, though the verdict is still much under debate. Lord knows, messing around with genes is nothing new. Ever since we learned to tame plants, we've tampered with the genes that nature gave them. For something close onto fourteen—not one or two but *fourteen*—millennia, we have applied unnatural selection to our grains and greens, choosing those that are most vigorous, productive, flavorful, and resistant to diseases and pests. A prime example is that of the brassicas, the cabbages, that over the centuries have been transformed by gardeners and farmers into botanically identical but otherwise immensely diverse-looking plants, each with a flavor of its own: kale and cauliflower, broccoli, collards, brussels sprouts, and all the rest. As master gardener William Woys Weaver says, "Genetic change is inevitable." He cites pictorial evidence: wall paintings at Pompeii, for example, and ancient herbals that show earlier varieties of the flowers, shrubs, and vegetables that we know today. Of course, abominations have occurred along with the triumphs: Our opinionated kind also selects for the wrong reasons—because plants are pretty or because they ship well. The upshot takes myriad forms, from hard, tasteless tomatoes to all-out attack by kudzu, once thought to be neatly, sweetly decorative, a good vine to wind up a trellis and shade a porch. As for the new breed of genetically modified organisms, plants into which genes have been inserted, I think it marvelous that essential foodstuffs, like corn and soy, can be grown with built-in resistance to the bugs and blights that would otherwise reduce the harvest, not to mention killing them. We do not know the long-term consequences of what we do, but given the hunger and impoverishment endemic among much of humankind, the risks are worthwhile. As usual in the case of large uncertainties, some people have issued canards about the dangers of human interference with nature's bounty. Take the case of the monarch butterflies: It is said that they are poisoned by the Bt-containing pollen of corn genetically altered to kill corn borers. The report is not false, but all the experiments with monarch larvae and this pollen took place in a laboratory at Cornell University. And the report scants some important facts. It doesn't take into account the biology of monarch butterflies. It only speaks to the human condition: what we think, what we feel without thinking about an insect that we find beautiful and, thus, desirable. Truth is that monarch butterflies are to be found only on the periphery of cornfields, and then only if milkweed, the sole food of their larvae, is available. Milkweed is certainly not found in the middle of an agribusiness corn patch. There will be casualties among the larvae at the edge of an engineered field, but hardly enough to exterminate the species. It's risky anyhow to be a butterfly, a fragile creature exposed all its life to potential calamity—wind, hard rains, and predators. But when I come down on the side of genetic engineering, I do not mean to say that diversity should not be treasured, that heritage seeds should not be saved so that old gene pools are on hand for the tapping should experiments fail, should potatoes and corn be wiped out again by blight.

At this point in human history it doesn't matter that we weren't meant to garden. We can't stop mucking around with earth and plants. We can't stop trying to reconnect with a world greater than our finite selves. There's something downright seductive about grubbing in earth and growing our own food. We may not have been designed to farm, but surely people have always gotten religion and dirtied their hands messing around with earth and plants. I imagine a woman in the times before the Bronze Age: She notes the belly-filling qualities of some wild food and finds, most likely by accident, that spilled seeds will sprout; all she needs to do is remember where they fell to earth. Or she digs up an attractive plant as she grubs out something else; along with edible tubers, it goes home in her gathering sack, but she tosses it out: Behold, it touches earth, takes root, and rises once again. Initial wonder turns to self-assurance; the next time she sees the same perennial in the wild, she digs it up on purpose, for the pure joy of doing so, and resets it by her doorstep.

To be sure, growing fruits and vegetables is hard, grubby, exhausting, back-bending, sometimes dispiriting labor. It's not a product of summer country where the living is easy. It's certainly not Edenic.

Eden was a natural garden, not one made by humans. But oh, we've been granted the ability to touch earth again and again to gain strength, to sustain flesh and spirit, to keep our bodies hale and our imaginations vital. We can do it ourselves!

Earth also heals. A story told some years ago by A. W. Jefferies, Jeff to his friends, comes to mind; it arose from his experience as a psychiatrist at one of Virginia's state mental hospitals. Before deinstitutionalization of the mentally ill became de rigueur in the 1960s, long-term patients at the hospital worked a large truck garden and ran a dairy operation, both of which supplied goods to the county and its two cities. These enterprises ended when the new regime of short stays and rapid patient releases came rolling in, pushing past practices out of the way. The results, said Jeff, were nowhere more visible than in the lack of work for those hospitalized. The patients' sense of productivity—and of social as well as commercial usefulness—vanished; violent behavior and outright psychosis increased hideously. To lose touch with earth was, for these people, to lose touch altogether.

But what of those in the larger world who do not—cannot—touch earth? All too many people are locked into inner cities, where objects common to the hand are things like plastic, concrete, and hypodermic needles. I remember a child, a seven-year-old girl, who long ago came from the Bronx to visit our next-door neighbors in Connecticut under the auspices of a fresh-air program. She stayed with them for two weeks, and for two weeks she screamed in terror when she saw things like butterflies and puppies. In her mind, attuned to familiar urban wildlife, all insects were roaches; all animals, rats. It may also be that soil and vegetables, flowers too, did not exist for her; they were utterly outside her tender but ravaged experience.

To touch earth is to draw on the healing powers of planting and tending vegetables. But no matter what we plant and when, be it in accord with the lunar dictates or just as the inclination strikes, the gardening game is a great gamble: *O Fortune, like the moon, ever-changing, waxing, waning.* And the fortune of the garden is as changeable as the weather, as subject to uncertainty and random blows as are human affairs. And, sure as the earth rolls through spring into summer, there will be losses. Some will be due to human carelessness or inanition, like the disking that wiped out the horse-radish or my all-too-frequent failure to weed thoroughly enough; others will be wrought by natural disasters, like the long drought that did in 1998's tomatoes, the midsummer hurricane of 1996 that lashed Garden Field with a killing salt spray, or the hurricane of August 1999 that toppled the pole limas. Every summer heat will sit on the land like a huge, broody bird. And there are always ravenous worms and beetles, along with the silent, subterranean minions of Robigus, the god of blight. Why keep on, why spend energy and time and sweat when losses are certain?

Things change, time spirals on. The ever-cockadoodling rooster and his battery of hens are gone, killed by dogs (I never thought I'd miss his ardent crowing). The High Cockalorum has moved away, hallelujah! The people who bought her house are down-to-earth and generous. The Point's population burgeons: Another doublewide has been plopped onto a lot in the third tier inland from the river; another house rises behind the hedgerow that conceals our place. The Chief has considerably expanded the garden in New Field, all the better to hold three dozen tomato bushes, plus some heirloom indeterminates—purple-red 'Brandywine' and also 'Big Rainbow', yellow streaked with red inside and out. Becky grew the latter from seeds that she had saved and planted in potting soil enriched with manure from her chickens. And I have just acquired a packet of New Zealand spinach seeds. I had expected something dainty. No, the hard seeds resemble kernels of dried corn, flat on one end, somewhat pointed on the other, and they're just as big.

But change, for all that it is constant in human life, does not affect everything. Our hopes are immune. We do replant: The horseradish will rise again from roots supplied by Becky and Dennis. We do fight back: When the soil of Garden Field turned out to harbor both verticillium and fusarium, fungi that clog tomatoes' ability to take up water and then wilt the bejesus out of them, we moved the tomato patch to New Field, where it thrives. And we plan to solarize the earth in Garden Field, putting down and anchoring a layer of clear plastic twelve feet wide and a hundred feet long. With this arrangement, the sun shines down and bakes the soil six inches down, cooking not only the fungi but also the weed seeds, soil arthropods, and nematodes right out of existence. *We plan*—brave words that may contain no substance, given our all-too-frequent inanition and increasing decrepitude. The question arises again and with increasing urgency as the years go by: Why persist?

For many reasons, some lightweight, others substantial. To begin with, gardening has become a habit. Without the plants, summer would stretch ahead like a desert to slog across. We need the green, the flavors, the earthy smells, the rustle and tumble of life that pervade the venture. More than that, growing vegetables—not just vegetables but flowers, too, and planting trees—means participation in *religio,* reconnection. It means searching for sense in the turning of the earth, in both of its turnings. The one near at hand is the tilling of the soil to prepare it for new seeds and to keep Antaios's children from barging in too deeply. The other, near, far, and all-encompassing, is the turning of the planet through the universe, day succeeding night, cold yielding in its time to warmth, and the whole cycle rolling on year in, year out, over and over again like a great wheel. We look to gardening for an enduring logic, a reasonableness, an overarching harmony, amid the random assaults and discordances of being alive.

It's Thomas Jefferson who speaks most truly for us. Writing in 1811 to the noted portrait painter Charles Willson Peale, he says:

> I have often thought that if heaven had given me a choice of my position and calling, it should have been on a rich spot of earth, well watered, and near a good market for the productions of the garden. No occupation is so delightful to me as the culture of the earth, and no culture comparable to that of the garden. Such a variety of subjects, some one always coming to perfection, the failure of one thing repaired by the success of another, and instead of one harvest a continued one throughout the year. . . . But though an old man, I am but a young gardener.

He was sixty-eight when he wrote this letter. As I write in the present day, I realize that the Chief and I are only a year shy of that mark. And in the nearly two decades that we've been growing vegetables in the sandy loam of Great Neck Point, we've both aged out of spryness. We both went blimp, padding ourselves with unnecessary pounds when we stopped smoking in 1991 (but better fat and free than skinny and smoking). The Chief has dentures (which he does not wear), and heat does him in, robbing him of every last drop of energy. I still have more than my share of get-up-and-go, no matter the weather. I also have a left knee made of metal and plastic; it's somewhat stiff but far better than the old, painful, arthritic model.

To be sure, differences exist between our day and Jefferson's. But though we are not close to a market for our productions—nor do we grow our small crops for sale—many people share our bounty nonetheless, from family and friends to stray visitors and the UPS deliveryman. It goes without saying, of course, that we are exceedingly grateful that we need not cope with the tasks, like saving seeds, and with the unrelieved, un-air-conditioned exposure to summer's steamy heat that faced gardeners in Jefferson's day. The rest of what Jefferson says is gospel. The body ages, but the spirit retains a youthful resilience. Touching earth is more effective than any fountain of youth or cucumber poultice for keeping the senses vigorous and encouraging the sweet rage of imagination. As he says, perfection is ever imminent, and success does repair failure. Best of all, hope springs ever green, ever seductive in the gardener's heart.

APPENDIX

W. Atlee Burpee & Co.
300 Park Avenue
Warminster, PA 18991-0008
(800) 888-1447
www.burpee.com

The Cook's Garden
P.O. Box 535
Londonderry, VT 05148
Order Center: P.O. Box 5010
Hodges, SC 29653-5010
(800) 457-9703
www.cooksgarden.com

Ed Hume Seeds
P.O. Box 1450
Kent, WA 98035
http://humeseeds.com

Heirloom Seeds
P.O. Box 245
West Elizabeth, PA 15088-0245
(412) 384-0852
www.heirloomseeds.com

Johnny's Selected Seeds
1 Foss Hill Road
RR 1, Box 2850
Albion, ME 04910-9731
(207) 437-4301
www.johnnyseeds.com

Park Seed
1 Parkton Avenue
Greenwood, SC 29647-0001
(800) 845-3369
www.parkseed.com

Seeds of Change
P.O. Box 15700
Santa Fe, NM 87506-5700
(888) 762-7333
www.seedsofchange.com
gardener@seedsofchange.com

Shepherd's Garden Seeds
30 Irene Street
Torrington, CT 06790-6658
(860) 482-3638
www.shepherdseeds.com

Southern Exposure Seed Exchange
P.O. Box 460
Mineral, VA 23117
(540) 894-9480

The Thomas Jefferson Center
  for Historic Plants:
  Twinleaf Catalog
P.O. Box 316
Charlottesville, VA 22902
www.monticello.org/shop

NOTES

Full citations appear in the bibliography.

PLANTING BY THE MOON

Page 47 "A Riddle": Beam, 31.

47 Anciently, cabbages of every sort . . . cabbage tonics: Pliny, XX.xxxiii.78ff.

48 "greenish-white": Dove, 24.

51 "The new Moon": *The Old Farmer's Almanac,* 90.

53 *O Fortuna:* Whicher, 262.

THE LIVES OF THE VEGETABLES

Page 56 "foure graines": Harriott, 15.

58 "jellylike substance": National Gardening Association, 373.

60 "In Egypt and Barbary": Gerard, 344–5.

60 "The purple ones": Randolph, 108.

61 "The whole Plant is of a ranke": Gerard, 346.

61 The first report: sign in the kitchen garden of the Tryon Palace, seat of colonial government, New Bern, North Carolina.

62 "If a woman wants": Jong, 6.

62 "good poetry": Dove, 24.

63 "Ginnie peppers"; "grow the cods": Gerard, 365.

64 *reod,* which means "red": Grieve, 677.

64 there he credits radishes: Pliny, XIX.xvv.79.

64 "They cause belchings": Gerard, 239.

65 "pleasant to be eaten": Gerard, 1027.

65 "it serveth love matters"; "is more effectual": Gerard, 1029.

66 India perhaps: Spencer, 157.

66 Gerard notes nothing but: Gerard, 1219–20.

66 Of the grand array: Jefferson, 7.

67 Pliny, who devoted: Pliny, XIX.xli.145–51.

68   Calling it "Sperage": Gerard, 1111.

68   "Asparagus come to table": Jefferson, 576, 627, and elsewhere.

68   Pliny, who finds it a peculiar: Pliny, XIX.xxii.64.

68   Pliny also ascribes: Pliny, XX.v.10.

68   its seeds provide: Pliny, XX.iii.8.

69   "First of all, in the middle"; "doth perfectly cure": Gerard, 909–12.

71   "called by us, *Pompions*": Harriott, 14.

71   "the Virginian Macocke": Gerard, 919

FULL OF BEANS

Page 78   "For I have had too much": Frost, 69.

80   "Carbonized favas": Weaver, 4.

81   they were allied with the forces: Pliny, XVIII.xxx.117–9.

81   Still, science . . . defense against disease: Cochran and Ewald, 40.

82   "The Beane is windie meate"; "The fruits and cods of Kidney Beanes"; "neither toothsome nor wholesome": Gerard, 1209–11.

87   "Brasile Kidney Beane"; "in his ful bignesse"; "seeds of divers colours": Gerard, 1215.

88   And oh, the varieties he grew: Jefferson, throughout.

PARSLEY, SAGE, ROSEMARY, AND LEMON THYME

Page 94   in his *Herball:* Gerard, 1292–3.

94   "As for Rosmarine": More quoted by Grieve, 682.

96   image drawn by the Roman poet Virgi: Virgil, *Georgics* IV.180–1.

101   "Organy given in wine": Gerard, 667.

103   "It doth marvellously prevaile": Gerard, 577.

103   "an excellent water": Gerard, 766.

104   "watered satin": Catesby quoted by Feduccia, 109.

105 Pliny mentions it . . . a menstruating woman: Pliny, XIX.lvi.176ff.

106 "Dioscorides saith"; "the seed drunke"; "good for the heart": Gerard, 674.

107 "And so she ever fed it": Keats, "Isabella; or, The Pot of Basil," 425–30.

ANTAIOS'S CHILDREN

Page 109 "Soon, the labor": Virgil, *Georgics,* Book I, 150–4. Translation by JL.

115 "During most of his life;" "probably the finest": Green, 161.

122 "was gather'd very young": Beverly quoted by Heiser, 139.

126 the root's flavor is said to be: Weaver, 365.

129 "All ethics": Leopold, 203–4.

QUEEN MAB'S WAGGON

Page 136 "entertaining but has more to do": Hubbell, 61

140 I have been told . . . stink bug has traveled: Fichter, 70.

140 "What a delightful collection"; "masterpieces of elegant simplicity": Fabre, 79.

141 "a rich, bubbling down-sweep of tone": Cocroft, 54.

141 In one experiment . . . she may be found: Cocroft, 56.

143 other treatments suggested . . . an infusion of garlic: Carr, 117.

143 placing the skull of a horse: Pliny, XIX.lviii.180.

146 "O! then, I see, Queen Mab": Shakespeare, *Romeo and Juliet,* I.iv.53–71.

A BLOOMING OF GARDENERS

Page 152 "I do not see but the seeds": Thoreau, 198.

161 It may be that Tom's hot peppers: Spencer, 206.

176 "He who . . . fattens a pig": Spencer, 89.

FEASTS

Page 181   "To send up the beans whole": Randolph, 104.

TOUCHING EARTH

Page 203   studies made by the anthropologist . . . fish and mammoths
there: Larsen summarized by Allport, 220–31.

204   "Consider the variety": Pliny, XVIII.i.2.

205   "Genetic change": Weaver, 4.

210   "I have often thought": Jefferson, 461.

BIBLIOGRAPHY

Agricultural Research Service, United States Department of Agriculture. *Common Weeds of the United States.* New York: Dover Publications, Inc., 1971. First published as *Selected Weeds of the United States* by the Government Printing Office, 1970.

Allport, Susan. *The Primal Feast: Food, Sex, Foraging, and Love.* New York: Harmony Books, 2000.

Beam, Jeffery. *Visions of Dame Kind.* Winston-Salem, NC: The Jargon Society, 1995.

Berenbaum, May R. *Ninety-Nine Gnats, Nits, and Nibblers.* Urbana and Chicago: University of Illinois Press, 1989.

———. *Ninety-Nine More Maggots, Mites, and Munchers.* Urbana and Chicago: University of Illinois Press, 1993.

Betts, Edwin Morris, annotator. *Thomas Jefferson's Garden Book, 1766–1824.* Philadelphia: The American Philosophical Society, 1992. Reprint.

Bradley, Fern Marshall, ed. *Garden Answers: Vegetables, Fruits, and Herbs.* Emmaus, Penn.: Rodale Press, 1995.

Carr, Anna. *Color Handbook of Garden Insects.* Emmaus, Penn.: Rodale Press, 1979.

Cochran, Gregory, and Paul W. Ewald. "High-Risk Defenses: The Body's Self-Destructive Assault against Infection." *Natural History* 108, No. 1 (February 1999), 40–5.

Cocroft, Rex. "Thornbug to Thornbug: The Inside Story of Insect Song." *Natural History* 108, No. 8 (October 1999), 52–7.

Coombes, Allen J. *Dictionary of Plant Names.* Portland, Ore.: Timber Press, 1994.

Dove, Rita. *The Yellow House on the Corner.* Pittsburgh: Carnegie Mellon University Press, 1989.

Duncan, Wilbur H., and Marion B. Duncan. *Seaside Plants of the Gulf and Atlantic Coasts: From Louisiana to Massachusetts, Exclusive of Lower*

Peninsula Florida. Washington, D.C., and London: Smithsonian Institution Press, 1987.

———. *Wildflowers of the Eastern United States*. Athens and London: The University of Georgia Press, 1999.

Environmental Protection Agency. "Weedlaws." *The John Marshall Law Review* 26, No. 4 (summer 1993).

Evans, Hazel, with Gloria Nicol. *The Herb Basket: An Illustrated Companion to Herbs*. Gadalming, Surrey, U.K.: CLB International, 1996.

Fabre, Jean Henri. *The Passionate Observer: Writings from the World of Nature*. San Francisco: Chronicle Books, 1998.

Feduccia, Alan, ed. *Catesby's Birds of Colonial America*. Chapel Hill and London: The University of North Carolina Press, 1985.

Fichter, George M. *Insect Pests*. New York: Golden Press, 1966.

Fleischman, Paul. *Seedfolks*. New York: HarperCollins Publishers, Inc., 1997.

Frost, Robert. *The Poetry of Robert Frost*. Edward Connery Latham, ed. New York: Holt, Rinehart and Winston, 1969.

Gadsby, Patricia. "How Now, Sow Bug?" *Discover* 20, No. 8 (August 1999), 64–7.

Gerard, John. *The Herball, or Generall Historie of Plantes*. The Complete 1633 Edition as Revised and Enlarged by Thomas Johnson. New York: Dover Publications, Inc., 1975. An unabridged replication of the work originally published by Adam Islip, Joice Norton and Richard Whitakers, London, 1633.

Green, J. Reynolds. *A History of Botany in the United Kingdom from the Earliest Times to the End of the 19th Century*. London and Toronto: J. M. Dent & Sons Limited; New York: E. P. Dutton & Co., 1914.

Grieve, Mrs. M. *A Modern Herbal*. New York: Dover Publications, Inc., 1971. Reprint of a work originally published by Harcourt, Brace & Company, 1931.

Harriott, Thomas. *A Briefe and True Report of the New Found Land of Virginia*. New York: Dover Publications, Inc., 1972.

Haughton, Claire Shaver. *Green Immigrants: The Plants That Transformed America*. New York and London: Harcourt Brace Jovanovich, 1978.

Heiser, Charles B., Jr. *The Fascinating World of the Nightshades: Tobacco, Mandrake, Potato, Tomato, Pepper, Eggplant, Etc.* New York: Dover Publications, Inc., 1987.

Hilyard, Paul. *The Book of the Spider: From Arachnophobia to the Love of Spiders*. New York: Random House, 1994.

Hubbell, Sue. *Broadsides from the Other Orders: A Book of Bugs*. New York: Random House, 1993.

———. *Waiting for Aphrodite: Journeys into the Time before Bones*. Boston and New York: Houghton Mifflin Company, 1999.

Jong, Erica. *Fruits and Vegetables*. New York: Holt, Rinehart and Winston, 1968, 1970, 1971.

Kaston, B. J. *How to Know the Spiders*, 3rd ed. Dubuque, Iowa: William C. Brown Company, Publishers, 1978.

Kincaid, Jamaica. *My Garden (Book)*. New York: Farrar Straus Giroux, 1999.

Kowalchik, Claire, and William B. Hylton, eds. *Rodale's Illustrated Encyclopedia of Herbs*. Emmaus, Penn.: Rodale Press, 1987.

Landau, Lois M., and Laura G. Myers. *Too Many Tomatoes, Squash, Beans, and Other Good Things: A Cookbook for When Your Garden Explodes*. New York: HarperCollins, 1976.

Lawson, John. *A New Voyage to Carolina*. Hugh Talmage Lefler, ed. Chapel Hill: The University of North Carolina Press, 1967.

Leopold, Aldo. *A Sand County Almanac: And Sketches Here and There*. New York: Oxford University Press, 1949.

Levi, Herbert W., and Lorna R. Levi. *A Guide to Spiders and Their Kin*. New York: Golden Press, 1968.

Manning, Phillip. *Islands of Hope: Lessons from North America's Great Wildlife Sanctuaries*. Winston-Salem, N.C.: John F. Blair, Publisher, 1999.

Martof, Bernard S., William M. Palmer, Joseph R. Bailey, and Julian R.

Harrison III. *Amphibians and Reptiles of the Carolinas and Virginia.* Chapel Hill: The University of North Carolina Press, 1980.

Millspaugh, Charles F. *American Medicinal Plants.* New York: Dover Publications, Inc., 1974. Reprint of *Medicinal Plants,* published by John C. Yorston & Company, Philadelphia, 1892.

Milne, Lorus, and Margery Milne. *National Audubon Society Field Guide to North American Insects and Spiders.* New York: Alfred A. Knopf, 1980.

National Gardening Association. *Dictionary of Horticulture.* New York: Penguin Books, 1994.

Nybakken, Oscar E. *Greek and Latin in Scientific Terminology.* Ames: The Iowa State University Press, 1959.

The Old Farmer's Almanac. Dublin, N.H.: Yankee Publishing, Inc., 2000.

Pliny. *Natural History.* Vol. V. Translated by H. Rackham. Cambridge, Mass.: Harvard University Press, 1950.

———. *Natural History.* Vol. VI. Translated by W. H. S. Jones. Cambridge, Mass.: Harvard University Press, 1951.

Preston-Mafham, Rod, and Ken Preston-Mafham. *Spiders of the World.* New York: Facts on File Publications, 1984.

Randolph, Mary. *The Virginia Housewife Or, Methodical Cook.* New York: Dover Publications, Inc., 1993. A Facsimile of an Authentic Early American Cookbook (1824).

Rodale Garden Press Books. *Weed-Ending Secrets: What Weeds Don't Want You to Know.* Emmaus, Penn.: Rodale Press, Inc., 1997.

Rombaugh, Lon J. "The Garden's Uninvited Guests." *Gardening How-To* Vol. 4, No. 3 (May/June 1999), 38–45.

Simmons, Amelia. *The First American Cookbook.* New York: Dover Publications, Inc., 1984. A Facsimile of *American Cookery,* 1796.

Smith, A. W. *A Gardener's Handbook of Plant Names: Their Meanings and Origins.* Mineola, N.Y.: Dover Publications, Inc., 1997.

Smith, Miranda, and Anna Carr. *Rodale's Garden Insect, Disease & Weed Identification Guide.* Emmaus, Penn.: Rodale Press, 1988.

Spencer, Colin. *The Vegetable Book.* New York: Rizzoli, 1995.

Thoreau, Henry David. *Wild Fruits.* Bradley P. Dean, ed. New York: W. W. Norton & Company, 2000.

Viney, Michael. "Long Live the Weeds." *Natural History* 108, No. 3 (April 1999), 104.

Virgil. *The Eclogues and Georgics.* Translated by C. Day Lewis. Garden City, N.Y.: Anchor Books, 1964.

Weaver, William Woys. *Heirloom Vegetable Gardening: A Master Gardener's Guide to Planting, Seed Saving, and Cultural History.* New York: Henry Holt and Company, 1997.

Whicher, George F. *The Goliard Poets: Medieval Songs and Satires in a New Translation.* Privately printed, 1949.